SHE IS ALL BUSINESS

How to Build an Eight-Figure Empire by
Allowing God to be the CEO

Terry Rasner

ISBN: 979-8-9939738-2-1 Paperback
ISBN: 979-8-9939738-3-8 ebook

I want to thank my mother, Christine,
for instilling in me a love of God,
the power of prayer,
and the strength of a warrior.

My daughter, Sarah Elayne,
my princess of light, who gave me
the full meaning of life and the ability to see
supernaturally.

My grandson, Howard Edward Zink IV,
who is his grandma's anchor
in so many profoundly spiritual ways.

My husband, John,
who has always been my wingman.

And lastly, to all those who believed in me.
I love you all!

Contents

Big Vision of She Is All Business...1

Dignity, Courage, and Achievement 3

Homeless in Houston...17

Hanging with the Monks in Big Sur 31

Loving the Source of Pain and Suffering...............................51

My First Encounter in Hearing God's Voice: A Miracle Was

Breathed!..61

Your Mom, My Mom 73

When Angels Visit! 93

What Do Santa Claus and Christ Have in Common? Me! 99

My Hunka Wunka!..111

Author's Foreword

Seems like I wasted no time pursuing my first million dollars, though I was on the very slow track, as written in the Author's Foreword of the 1st Edition of She Is All Business. And although this is the Foreword to the 2nd Edition of *She Is All Business*, I want to honor again the memory of how my entrepreneurial adventure began.

I was eight years old, and my cousin Gina and I would go to the local market and buy $1 worth of Brach's candies in bulk and then sell them for a nickel each on the corner of Utah Street where we lived in Carson City, Nevada. There was hard work involved in buying and wrapping the candies for sale, counting the money, keeping records, paying the bills, and sharing the profit, but what most mattered was that we were young entrepreneurs, and **we were a success!**

Fast forward to 2017, three years since the release of the 1st Edition of *She Is All Business*, and **we are a success!** The management team and I needed to release a 2nd Edition to satisfy the pent-up demand for re-exposure to the services, philosophy, and goodwill the "*She Is All Business* Enterprise" offers the public.

I'll begin with the nominally priced subscription to my Basic Business Academy Course, which, upon completion, unlocks unending website connections, training opportunities, and networking options. Women of all ages have taken online courses we've piloted over the years, and the Basic Business Academy Course is most favored for the self-discovery it affords in one's complete privacy. You can learn plenty that you can take with you to your next office meeting, job interview, or business luncheon. So, enjoy our expanded website offerings and added insights!

Much bigger to Dr. John, however, is our corporate commitment to what he calls "Principled Leadership in the content area of **Transformational Thinking**." Dr. John, who blogs on our website along with me, has for years encouraged us to "raise the corporate bar" by bringing **Transformational Thinking** to the forefront of our Corporate model, and including it more boldly in the 2nd Edition, in our Consulting Contracts, in my Public Speaking engagements, and in our future-casting for creating change in communities and organizations.

We agree with Dr. John, and I'd like to quote a passage from Chapter 1 on our conceptualization of **Transformational Thinking**. It is genuinely a "life-shaping" orientation — one that some may find too challenging to follow without guidance and counsel. This is precisely where our consulting services come into play, especially when **transformations** are strategically important to business success or survival.

"Foremost, **TT** is about constant change in you: **a change that's integrated in body, mind, heart, and spirit.** What's truly fascinating about **TT** is that **you really need to understand and accept your own conflict and contradiction.** You've got to begin doing so from the point of reference of your spirituality, as this aspect of your whole person will drive you most powerfully and reliably.

It is from the starting point of your spirituality that you need to project your understanding that the whole world around you is in a state of transformation at all times and that you have an intuitive connection to this transformation!"

We know and accept transformation and change as constant; it's not fight or flight, but **know and flow!**

Remember what my mother used to say about me, "That girl is all business!"

It was fitting that my mother would be the one to anoint me with the "all business" title because God most certainly anointed my mother. My confession throughout my book is plainly and most certainly that without God's teachings, blessings, and anointing, I could not have become the adult version of that twelve-year-old little girl, who is today, the woman blessed to be called: **She Is All Business**!

For a moment, and just before we move into Chapter 1, let me emphasize once again the importance and significance of the subtitle of my book: **How God & the Supernatural Can Guide You to Prosperity & Success.** Those words are no accident, nor were they ever intended to be taken any way but quite literally. Please understand, God and the Supernatural – in thought, word & action – are all about the offices and work areas of *She Is All Business*; this fact of corporate life is immutable, and this alone generates solidarity, and in turn a fidelity   to   our commitment to maintain a level of prosperity and success that's in balance with our witness to God and the supernatural.

There are undoubtedly many messages in my book, but above all, there is but one—that is, until I understood and believed with all my heart and soul that God was the message of my success and blessings, all the wonderful and exciting concepts I learned about business and people meant nothing. So, in the chapters that follow, you'll not read about how to build a multimillion-dollar enterprise, but how to recognize the work of God in your life through His actions, His Words, and the Holy Spirit. For you see—*and must know*—God is always on the *move* in our lives; make way for His leadership, and your life as an entrepreneur and successful business owner will be a witness to how well you listen and are obedient to God!

When my daughter, Sarah, read my book, she suggested I consider the subtitle "From God's Intern to His Trusted CEO". Let her words carry you through this book.

1

Big Vision of She Is All Business

Think of this businesswoman as the CEO who looks first to God and then moves in accordance with the urgings of the Holy Spirit. This businesswoman will be the catalyst to creating your million-dollar dream (and then helping you bring it to life!). She is a dream-maker who's not afraid to pray or take risks of faith, while using both radical and unconventional methods/systems for both personal and business applications.

When you embrace her creative spirit as nurtured by her faith in God, neither *she nor God will ever disappoint you*—though you may find yourself going in a different direction than you planned. Understand, this Holy Spirit–inspired businesswoman appears at times to have the will of a wild mustang, unbridled, untamed, and free. *A Transformational Thinker*, she will take you to your highest level of self-mastery...if you give her the reins! She is the persona of extraordinary strength; give her a try and know if you're right with God, you can be certain He's got your back.

Carry this lasting image in your mind and embrace the essence that She Is All Business brings to your life; hold on and give her the reins. Indeed, imagine yourself as God's intern!

2

Dignity, Courage, and Achievement

(How God used nunchakus to reveal the physicality of my inner core!)

In my story, the discussions and examples that follow make references to these themes:

- *Dignity* (and I do believe God had dignity in mind when He created women) - how disgusting it is to dishonor the *dignity* of women completely, and respectfully, the *dignity* of their spouses and life partners.

- *Fear*—truly out of *fear*, I had been holding his gun as firmly as I could for sixty seconds. I heard some call him a punk, yet to me, he was physically threatening, with a mouth on him spewing filthy sexual smack talk intended, I surmised, to play with my mind and keep me off balance.

- *Courage*—all I could think about was "this is my call to *courage*"—that was it. As I approached the ring of combat, I began hyperventilating, worried I wouldn't

3

have enough air to breathe. I had always been a bit claustrophobic, so naturally, my anxiety was growing even as my call to *courage* was keeping pace with my knowing under these circumstances that God would be in the ring with me, and that's a tremendous advantage!

- *Achievement*—I worked very hard in POST (Police Officers Standards and Training) Academy and earned an award at the 1990 Academy graduation for my *achievements* in physical fitness and overall skills performance.

MY STORY

About the fourth week of Peace Officer Standards and Training (POST), it was weapon retention training. Okay, this was a while ago. The class had thirty-six men and six women, only three of whom had gotten this far in POST. Police work was a guy's gig, and I was paired up with a male trainee (who thought a bit much of himself). As we came face-to-face for a physical and technical weapons retention engagement challenge, he began whispering what could only be called "phone sex" talk to me. Get the picture: I have my hands locked on his wooden pistol, preparing to wrestle it from him, and he's saying he could smell the sweet perfume on my body and other pointed comments... blah blah blah, more on him later in the story.

Growing up, I was surrounded by a male family that worked in law enforcement. My father was a sergeant who was later elected sheriff of the State Capital City of Nevada, Carson City. My uncle was a sergeant, and my grandfather was a retired guard at the state's maximum-security prison. As you might imagine, police talk was common at family gatherings.

In my early teens, when my father was sheriff, he subscribed to a professional national crime magazine featuring

4

unsolved murders in the US. For me and my three older brothers, it was forbidden reading. Yes, you're right; the temptation to read something forbidden was way too inviting, even for a teenage Christian girl whose mother would have spanked my bottom if she knew. The fascination was too great; I figured out its monthly delivery date, fetched it from the mailbox, looked at it from cover to cover, and then put it back in the mailbox as if it had that day been delivered. My interest in crime and criminal investigations led me to pursue a criminal justice minor in college. It didn't hurt that if I happened to be at the right place at the right time, my sheriff father would let me ride with him on crime scene calls, further whetting my appetite for this field of study.

These crime scene calls introduced me to all sorts of death and affliction perpetrated on humans by other humans. As a young Christian, it was unsettling to think that life meant so little to some that they had no remorse when swiping it from another. Worse, when taking the life or limb of a mother or father of young children. The "color purple" wasn't mystical or romantic on these crime scenes, but the color of people who had been killed or murdered.

I marveled at what people would do to one another. I saw all sorts of victims of vicious crimes and victims of crimes of passion. Often, these crimes were essentially a mystery until we arrived on the scene. Why I wasn't more bothered, I don't know, though a few scenes are etched in my memory.

One of these is of a heavyset man who had a full beard and a fatal seizure in his small apartment kitchen. During the seizure, his belt loop somehow got stuck on the refrigerator door. Apparently, as he went down, his belt loop tethered to the refrigerator, keeping him from falling entirely to the floor, and all that touched the floor was his head and upper torso.

Picture this: there he was, his legs and lower body held up by the refrigerator, and his head smashed on the floor in a pool of blood. When the investigators lifted his head off

5

the floor, there was plenty of blood, and rigor mortis had set in, and to a kid, he looked like the Hollywood Wolfman. It was bizarre and disturbing.

But then, there was a woman who jumped out of an airplane to commit suicide, and what was gross about finding her dead was that all we found was her head inside her helmet. The rest of her body?

Nevada's high country is home to coyotes and mountain lions. Was there ever a dull moment at these crime scenes? Apparently not to me; I got hooked and wanted to work in this field.

At thirty, I achieved my goal. I earned my Bachelor of Arts from the University of Nevada, Reno, and was enrolled in POST, a 16-week program held at the Highway Patrol Police Academy. We had to live on campus for the training. The place was so cultlike that the instructors controlled every aspect of your life. They could make or break you, and they made sure you knew it! At the time, I was working as an undercover enforcement agent for the Nevada Gaming Control Board. I had the swing shift beat for the entire Nevada-side Lake Tahoe gaming enterprises, and this academy training was necessary if I wanted to secure my career as an enforcement agent.

Recall I mentioned the world of police work was a guy's gig at the time I was in enforcement, and I'm half embarrassed to share something despicable I've lived with and that's haunted me for years. I've always wondered if I felt compelled to uphold some informal "insider's police code"—by keeping my mouth shut. I think the biggest challenge for Christians is weighing questionable and troublesome insider practices of one's employer against the common good and what I now know as the "conscience of Christ." Time for me to trample the memory of a despicable insider practice to ensure that in no way I endorse it!

Understand, I covered the Nevada-side Lake Tahoe gaming establishments, including many world-famous casino properties. For the most part, my enforcement activities were routine and relatively predictable, and generally, casino staff were cooperative. However, something very sinister and repugnant was happening nightly unbeknownst to casino patrons and staff alike. There were "eyes in the sky" and "elsewhere" all over casinos, and these "eyes" were cameras snapping surveillance photos.

Fair enough, you say—agreed, we needed surveillance to detect cheating and other illegal gaming practices. Still, this type of surveillance was inappropriate and frankly despicable.

While very appropriate gaming surveillance was being conducted, persons with the authority to do so were using the cameras to zoom in on women's private areas. Cameras were trained to peer down at women's low-cut blouses and dresses, or to look straight on at women wearing see-through garments. I know, such curiosity happens all the time and is on every newsstand, but in this case, the photos of women patrons were kept and displayed in a very private collection that was passed around to men for pleasure and entertainment!

At the beginning of the chapter, I expressed my belief that God had dignity in mind when He created women. Frankly, this practice in my then profession completely dishonored the dignity of women and, respectfully, the dignity of their spouses and life partners. Do you have any such memories from your early jobs or career choices? They're a bit haunting until they're finally released!

BACK TO THE SIXTEEN WEEK POST ACADEMY

My Gaming Control Board Enforcement position required me to complete POST. It was a tough haul, but two other women and I prevailed and graduated. I worked very hard in POST and earned an award at the 1990 Academy graduation for my achievements in physical fitness and overall skills performance. Yes, I was proud of my achievement awards, but graduation from POST was the culmination of sixteen weeks of passing many kinds of tests that were both physically and emotionally grueling. I recall the sense of my muscles and nerves always in a heightened state of alert, needing to keep a firm grip on my emotions. And why? Because I was one of three women in a man's world at POST, and we were put on warning that there were predators in the academy who might, for any number of egoistic reasons, try to take us down.

I was a single mother when I was in POST and were it not for my mother's love and willingness to come and stay with me, I couldn't have provided my daughter, Sarah, the loving and nurturing support she deserved while I was completing POST at the academy. My mother's presence provided Sarah with the stability and consistency in her life that ensured her safety, access to school and friends, and my sanity. And my mother's daily prayers of intercession for me and my success with POST, I'm sure, made it the success it was; thanks, Mom!

The pressures of being a single mom and the remembrance of losing my son several years prior and not spending nights at home with my daughter during academy training were no picnic, but if I was to evolve in my career, it was nonetheless a necessity. If I did not graduate POST, I would lose my job, period. Forget the career aspirations. When I reflect on this time of my life, it's hard to imagine the pressure I placed on myself; oops, but when I put this in the context of how this *She Is All Businesswoman* evolved from these early experiences, it makes perfect sense!

About halfway through POST, my roommate, a woman from Las Vegas, was dismissed. She could not pass one of the tests required to advance, and we were given only one chance. When we learned a new skill, we would practice and practice until we mastered it or it mastered us! So that brings us back to where this story began on an earlier page of this chapter.

As intended in the academy, we were randomly assigned partners for weapons retention training. It was stressed repeatedly   how   vital it was to effectively learn and demonstrate one's understanding of and ability to retain one's weapons in any given challenging situation. *I believe the*

8

statistic cited at the time was that 10 percent of the time, officers are killed by their own weapons in criminals' hands.

I was assigned to partner up with a man from Las Vegas, *the trainee I referred to as thinking a bit too much of himself.* He was actually a few inches taller than I and looked to be about twenty-five pounds heavier. The scenario for the exercise was cast in "play acting" (but play for real) roles where your partner was your enemy (and you his), and the whole exercise revolved around you protecting and retaining your weapon and not surrendering it to your enemy. For the exercise, you and your partner would take turns protecting your weapons while the other tried to disarm you.

For the exercise, we used wooden replicas of .38-caliber and 9-millimeter pistols. They were the exact shape and size of the handguns we carried on the job. The instructor blew the whistle, and we moved in on each other. I grabbed his gun as it was pointed at me. He grinned, and the "phone sex" talk began: *I can just smell your sweet perfume...*and more unprintable comments!

Truly out of fear, I had been holding his gun as firmly as I could for sixty seconds. I heard some call him a punk, yet to me, he was physically threatening, with a mouth on him spewing filthy sexual smack talk intended, I surmised, to play with my mind and keep me off balance. He resisted my efforts to control his weapon, but I was no weakling, and he was no Tarzan. After another thirty seconds of this dynamic tension, I abruptly let go of the wooden pistol. His hands gripping the wooden pistol popped up, and the wooden pistol split his forehead wide open. He immediately dropped to the ground, writhing in pain, rolling side to side, cursing me, and bleeding profusely.

I went to the ground quickly before the instructor ran up to us and quietly whispered to him, "The next time, you better think twice before you talk to a woman like that! Shame on you." The exercise was immediately halted. I was shaken up a bit, and I was asked to calm down to clear my head. As I went to prayer (and did indeed calm down), he was taken by an ambulance to the emergency room for examination. In the end, he had to have six stitches to seal the cut, leaving him with a permanent scar on his forehead.

It was over, so I thought, yet another trainee told me that he was watching me during the remaining twelve weeks of POST—that vengeance and payback were now on his agenda! Clearly, there were times I was concerned about my safety, but I knew God had my back. Some of the other trainees had me (the single mother) believing he had put out a hit on me to mess me up. There was no question that he "had it out" for me, and his unspoken anger was apparent through his stalking behavior. As secure as I felt in God, I recognized his ever-present threat of reprisal during my final weeks at the academy could be launched at any time. Perhaps this fear could have been allayed had a word of apology or remorse over his actions or insulting language been offered. Instead, it was an unpredictable and ongoing game of cat and mouse, in which I avoided him and any opportunities for him or a couple of his buddies to even the score. Alas, as life would have it, with his stitches gone, our fight had yet to be finished.

All the POST students sat in the bleachers and watched as our peers battled each other in pairings called out by the instructors. We all watched battle after battle, and all along, I was wondering when I was going to be called. Curiously, I noted this trainee hadn't been called yet either. I wasn't born yesterday; yes, the plan was to have the two of us duke it out in the ring—the loser paying the price of humiliation for a final test before graduation. Sure, it was prearranged, and I suspect side bets were being made *to teach me a lesson about respect and a woman's proper place in the force.*

Our names were called, and out of the bleachers, we came. In this exercise, we were suited up in special combat suits—we called them marshmallow suits. He won the coin toss and selected a PT 24 stick (i.e., a metal bat)—we had all received one-day training and certification to use it. I was left with a pair of nunchakus. I had received sixty minutes of nunchakus training, and although it was not "expert usage" training, the training was sufficient to use the nunchakus to defend myself. However, in the padded suit, it seemed I couldn't even swing them to hit myself. Great, I had spent months dodging this trainee, and now it was him and me in a 10-foot diameter circular ring.

All I could think about was this is my call to courage— that was it. As I approached the ring, I began hyperventilating, worried I wouldn't have enough air to breathe. I had always been a bit claustrophobic, so naturally, my anxiety was growing as well, even as my call to *courage* was keeping pace! I thought back to my brief training with them and remembered playing like Bruce Lee. Yikes…I was in trouble.

We entered the circle glaring at each other, and when the whistle blew, initiating our battle, a light went off in my head. I started hyperventilating and perspiring profusely, thinking all along, *he must have been dreaming of this day to finally have the justice he sought to take me out literally!* Pow! In violation of POST Academy training rules, he hit me with his PT 24 in the head right at the start, then took a defensive position.

The next thing I remember was a zero-to-90 transformation of my mind from this pensive "oh yikes" stage *to a state of being personally outraged at his behavior, for which a mighty force within me emerged to "fight this dude" to the end.* I began swinging my arms like a windmill, though some described the movement of my arms and nunchakus more like aircraft propellers. I was out of my mind, I suppose, and the nunchakus became vicious weapons of a raving maniac as I started screaming at the top of my lungs and moving like a madwoman. I think the referee and fellow students pretty much agreed I beat the living daylights out of him. In fact, I don't recall another PT 24 stick strike from him, nor did I hear the whistle blow to stop my assault.

Should I have heard the whistle? Ah yeah, they said the referee blew it five times to get me to stop, and I recall several instructors trying to get close enough to me to yell,

"Stop! Stop! Stop!" Perhaps I was a bit out of control. Still, it was a relatively controlled environment, and over the years I've often retraced this episode to remind myself that we really need to trust our inner strength and creativity in unexpected situations. The truth is, we never know just how much inner strength and creativity we may need to exert in response to any given situation.

The long of the story is that I graduated from POST with honors. I can't deny how it has stuck with me since POST that *your courage grows and fear diminishes when you are up against something worth fighting for!* And as a corollary to this, I learned that *fear and anxiety never come out as expected in almost all situations,* and that it's critical to have anchors of support. For me, one such anchor is my belief in God and my trust in Him, and along with this, I know I must have a skill set from which I can draw physical strength and strategic advantage when confronted with challenges and unexpected scenarios.

CHALLENGES I OVERCAME

As I candidly assess this stage of my young career, I recognize that I was challenged to confront something insidious — an issue that persists in the marketplace, in company lunchrooms, and across the corporate world. *The challenge I had to overcome was maintaining my integrity while defending the dignity of women.*

The easiest thing for my career at the time would have been to join in the revelry over the surveillance photos. Sure, I could have gone along with the guys, uh-huh, *but the price I would have paid in my spirit and conscience would have been to jeopardize my own dignity. Suppose I had compromised my dignity and values. In that case, I believe it would have ultimately cost my daughter, Sarah, a price she'd have to bear as she grew older.*

You see, the challenge was not to turn away from the despicable images in silence, but to elevate my *dignity* and that of my daughter. By not screaming "foul" and maintaining our path as a single mother and daughter on the move, we went up the ladder to a life of self-sufficiency that valued the importance of women in the workplace and our value as consumers.

I had mentioned earlier in the chapter that *courage grows and fear is diminished when you are up against something worth fighting for...yes, most certainly the truth.* Clearly, there are all kinds of obstacles we need to overcome along the way of our lives—tons! Nevertheless, overcoming obstacles comes with the territory of most life twists and turns, and in doing so, we rally our spiritual, intrapersonal (i.e., deeply within our psychological framework), and even family resources. Yet as in my story, there was one obstacle. One that took on the character of a major challenge that stood squarely between my success and failure in my Gaming Control Enforcement career.

OVERCOMING YOUR OWN CHALLENGES

I've included this "Overcoming Your Own Challenges" section in most chapters to give you an opportunity to consider some tools I used to overcome my challenges and overcome your own challenges in life. In constructing this section, I've used a range of real-life examples of challenges we all face from time to time that are relevant to the themes discussed thus far.

What's something that "trips you out"? You know, a cause, a behavior, a belief, or an activity you personally find particularly important, and yet at times, you witness, hear, or read of others degrading or insulting others (maybe your friends or coworkers) who care about these things of importance, say animal rights. *It's tough when someone unwittingly uses their authority and on-the-spot nonsense*

13

rules to block you from exercising your passion about what's important to you or when you're ready to take a stand on principle alone.

YOUR TURN

- What's something that makes you get on your *She Is All Business* headset?

- What blocks you from experiencing your passion?

- Is it worth fighting for? Why? And who's for you and who's against you?

APPLYING TRANSFORMATIONAL THINKING (TT) TO YOUR LIFE TODAY

Without question, it's your understanding and appreciation of *Transformational Thinking* that will propel you to tremendous success and achievement in both your personal and professional lives, because, for most of us, they are two distinct yet interrelated lives. *Thus, the closing of each chapter will address opportunities to apply transformational thinking to your life that reflect the chapter's themes.*

Let's establish this book's working themes of what **Transformational Thinking** is all about. Foremost, **TT** is about constant change in you: *a change that's integrated in body, mind, heart, and spirit.* What's truly fascinating about TT is that *you really need to understand and accept your own conflict and contradiction.* You've got to begin to do so from the point of reference of your spirituality, as this aspect of your whole person will drive you most powerfully and reliably.

It is from the starting point of your spirituality that you need to project your understanding that the whole world around you is in a state of transformation at all times and that you have an intuitive connection to this transformation!

In the most profound sense of *TT*'s spirituality, you must accept that what's at play is your most negative, complaining self, your wonderful, happy self, your self-critical self, and your most creative self. But what's best about these aspects of you is that in the *TT* world, they collectively embody our God-given talents, gifts, and *passions*. As such, they fuel our efforts to change. If we view their Source accordingly, we afford others a clear understanding of our intentions, a certain degree of tolerance, and approach the *transformations* in our lives fervently, yet respectfully and honestly.

Bishop T. D. Jakes, of the Potter's House (megachurch) in Dallas, Texas, speaks of life as an ongoing process of transformation, something you're never completely done with. Bishop Jakes says it plain and simple: God's using him while God's continuing to transform him, but he's quick to point out that you've got to get rid of the "tired and old things" in you to make room for *transformation*. He refers to your present condition as not being real; instead, think of it as a process you're going through to get to the next place you're headed to in your life— that place where *transformation* equals a renewed mind and real change!

If others can't quite understand your behavior, thinking you're acting a bit out of character, smile and tell them you're listening to the call from your spirit within and you're ready to get on your *She Is All Business headset, and give her the reins to take you to that place of passion where God wants you to be!*

- Distinguish between the emotional, physical, and financial pressure *you place on yourself* versus those kinds of pressures placed on you by *others*. Under the microscope of *TT*, how have your responses to the pressures you placed on yourself prepared you for putting on your *She Is All Business* headset and pursuing *the integrated life changes* that'll give you

15

greater access to your God-given talents, gifts, and passions?

- Do not accept any talk from a man or acknowledge whistles from the street because accepting either degrades you as a woman! And if you ever get the opportunity to let a man know he ought not talk filthy sexual smack to a woman, assert your womanhood, and please quote me: "The next time, you better think twice before you talk to a woman like that!"

- When you put on your *She Is All Business* headset, know it also as a call to courage; remember that *courage grows and fear leaves when you are up against something worth fighting for!*

3

Homeless in Houston

(At least my mind thought I was)

In my story, the discussions and examples that follow make references to these themes:

- *Integrity*: Honestly, I couldn't justify the partying in my mind when my hard-earned money was paying for me to attend the conference to "learn and return" information for my staff who could not attend; it was like an *integrity* thing to me. I had prayed for this opportunity, and taking it lightly almost felt like an insult to God.

- *Humility*: I sank into the middle seat, only to be shunned by my seatmates as they shook their heads in that particular "What the heck is this?" I was pretty messed up; no sleep for almost twenty-four hours, scraps of food, alcohol, and I looked like something the cat dragged in from the rain. If they only knew I was a *She Is All Business* woman in training, and frankly, a believer who stumbled. Not a word from my mouth:

17

God's forgiveness and public humility were the best alternatives I had.

- *Transparency*: And his spirit knew he needed to continue to hang out near me to allow me to be *transparent* and more open-minded, seeking out his assistance. Heck, he might even have bought me my own burger, fries, and soft drink.

- *Resourcefulness*: Trip after return trip to the water fountain and the café, I couldn't bring myself to the point of agreeing that indeed, my hunger was real, and this food was the ticket to my *resourcefulness* in solving my immediate dilemma. It was just so unnatural for me, and while part of me couldn't bring myself to do it, I was willing to accept the horrific hunger pangs I was experiencing.

MY STORY

It wasn't like any other time I'd attended a conference for my profession. I was averaging a conference a month for two years; basically, the same routine except this time was different...very different! Each conference was like clockwork: going from classes or meetings scheduled throughout the day, eating on the run to make the most of my time, scoping out who I thought were the most influential in their respective areas of real estate, and sitting near them. Yes, I was in the throes of a then-booming real estate market and wanted to learn as much as I could. I sought networking, inside tips, and secrets of the trade from the biggest and the best in the industry.

My business was growing by leaps and bounds at the time. I read every book I could find on real estate and frequently listened to audiotapes on different industry topics. Taking a snapshot of my life, I was never far from attending a conference, reading or listening to teachings on real estate topics of interest, or mixing it up with industry leaders.

So, there I was in Dallas, at a conference like so many others, yet I found myself strangely distracted sitting that first morning in the general opening session of the conference. Oddly, at least for me, I sat there lost in my head, distracted and paying little attention to what was being said by the speakers. Ironically, as class ended on the final morning of the conference, I was invited to a party and dinner that evening. Hah, out popped my standard answer: *How kind of you, but no thanks.* They persisted, and I maintained what became my stubborn "No thanks." Honestly, I couldn't justify the partying in my mind when my hard-earned money was paying for me to attend the conference to "learn and return" information for my staff who could not attend. It was like an integrity thing to me; I had prayed for this opportunity, and taking it lightly almost felt like an insult to God. There was also a nagging thought that I'd be wasting my money, since at this time in my life, I was supporting my mother so she could live in her own home. And oh yeah, I had to catch a 4:00 a.m. shuttle to the airport.

That should have been enough, but then, one of the most important men in the group I belonged to came up and persuaded me to join him and the others. He played to the "people pleaser" in me by saying so nicely, "Oh, come on, you never join us. You always go to your room and stay there. Just two hours, I promise. One client, one drink, my treat...that's it, I promise."

Immediately, I start rationalizing my acquiescence: he was right, I never did go anywhere with any of them, and heck, two hours—what harm can that be? So, without hesitation, I agreed to go. We were told to meet in the valet area outside the hotel at 6:00 p.m. I was there early, waiting, half-thinking maybe I should skip it (that *integrity* thing again). I really didn't have the time.

About then, I heard a shout directed at me from a head popping out of a nearby long-stretched limo, "Come on, come on…" I could hear the loud rock music blaring from within the limo as I approached it, my inner voice is screaming, "Oh Lord, what am I getting into. Don't get in." But I think a pair of horns popped out of my head, and I smiled and jumped right in. It looked like the party had started hours earlier!

I joined a night-long tour of many famous local bars and restaurants, and to my surprise, I was having a great time. I couldn't imagine why I hadn't ever done this before. I sang karaoke, drank straight shots of tequila, and was partying like it was New Year's Eve 1999. It was getting close to me having   to get back to the hotel to finish packing and catch the shuttle…yes, at 4:00 in the morning so that I could catch my flight home! The weather was rainy and overcast in late June. I felt a bit queasy from probably drinking too much and eating too little. Add to that, Ms. Priss hadn't showered, brushed her teeth, or changed her clothes. Really, too little time for what had always been essentials for me, but not on this trip. Still, I had made it to the airport by the skin of my dirty white teeth.

While frantically packing, I accidentally put my phone charger in my suitcase. Over the airport intercom came the announcement: "Due to current low visibility and threatening weather   conditions in the area, all flights are currently suspended as all airlines are currently prohibited from takeoffs and landings." Not fifteen minutes later, it started hailing outside, and the sight and sound of hail pounding these buildings was something we rarely saw or heard of in Nevada.

I had a connecting flight to catch out of Gate A2, which I was going to miss as it had been cancelled. I, like a crowd of other travelers, was looking at all possible flight options we had as soon as Dallas reopened. After waiting in line for some while, I finally got to the front of the line. The attendant told me excitedly that if I hurried (meaning, if I was willing to run) across the airport, I could catch a connecting flight to Houston, and then catch a

Southwest Airlines flight to Reno. This all sounded good to me, and I took off running, looking like a female version of O.J. Simpson's famous airport commercials.

Of course, there were a few other differences: I was hungover, dehydrated, perspiring like crazy, and my hair was a frightful mess. Ah, but I made the flight, and when I climbed aboard, all that was left were middle seats. Huffing and perspiring, not a brush of makeup on my face, I was as white as a sheet, and I'm sure smelled a bit boozed up, though by then I was entirely sober. I sank into the middle seat, only to be shunned by my seatmates as they shook their heads in that certain, "What the heck is this?" I was pretty messed up; no sleep for almost twenty-four hours, scraps of food, alcohol, and I looked like something the cat dragged in from the rain. If they only knew I was a *She is All Business* woman in training, and frankly, a believer who stumbled. Not a word from my mouth; God's forgiveness and public humility were the best alternatives I had at my disposal. I was really messed up and an embarrassment to my Christianity.

I was thankful I was able to pray myself to sleep on the flight to Houston, where , upon landing , the first thing I did after getting off the plane was to race   to   the bathroom. I was sure I had my grooming essentials thrown together in my large purse, but after a frantic search in the bathroom, I realized that, in my packing frenzy, I had likely thrown them into my suitcase with my phone charger.

There I was, my flight to Reno about five hours away, and I was still not quite dealing with the reality of my circumstance. I thought I could always buy the products I needed, including some real food!

I realized I hadn't called my husband to apprise him of the grand adventure I had gotten myself into. I dove into my spacious purse to retrieve my phone; of course, it was dead. My phone charger was still asleep in my suitcase. As I approached the convenience store, I noticed the cell phone charging station was available. Cool! I picked up everything I needed at the little store and presented it to the cashier with my credit card. Moments later: "Ma'am, your card was not approved. Do you have another one you would like me to process?"

"That's impossible," I replied, a creature of habit, I always paid my entire credit card balance monthly. I knew I had used it the night before in Dallas. I guess I used it all over Dallas; my card was on "fraud alert". I asked to use her phone to call the card company; after all, I had plenty of time, but her company's policy prohibited such calls. I had no cash; I never carry it. I was thirsty, hungry, and tired, and while I had my Father in heaven, it now seemed like I was homeless in Houston.

As I left all the things I desperately wanted on the counter, I turned around to leave and saw this stranger in line staring at me like I was trash. It was like he was psyching into the cashier's thinking, and they were agreeing I was like trash. As the hours trailed on, so did my mind. I found myself focusing on my hunger pangs; they were real! I had never gone hungry - food was always available, and there was plenty. The water fountain I frequented at the airport became an interesting conversation starter for some good soul, as on one of my visits, I found napkins from the airport café placed on it.

Curious, I located the nearby café and quickly noticed that many food trays were lying around, with uneaten, even unwrapped food on them. I turned away and left, only to return later to find even more food trays and uneaten, unopened food. My mind started playing games with me: *Those items, unfinished sandwiches, chips, cookies, and the like were left there for you, Terry. You're hungry, eat them!*

Return trip after return trip to the water fountain and the café, I couldn't bring myself to the point of agreeing that indeed, my hunger was real, and this food was the ticket to my resourcefulness in solving my immediate dilemma. It was just so unnatural for me, and while part of me couldn't bring myself to do it, I was willing to accept the horrific hunger pangs I was experiencing. Hmm? Big disconnect; the pangs only increased, and I knew I had no money.

The whole experience prompted me to review how I had gotten there, and as quickly as that, I felt defeated and stupid over what I had done the night before in Dallas. I just retreated to a row of seats well away from the water fountain and café, done with the temptations and mental circus I had created for myself. Then out of nowhere, what you might characterize as a classic gothic individual with longish, almost greasy dark hair wearing dark clothes sat down one seat away from me. He had pierced ears in which he wore a pair of plugs, a pierced eyebrow with a ring in it, eyeliner, tattoos, assorted facial tattoos, rings on his fingers, and fingernails painted black.

I glanced at him, and he returned an accommodating smile as he seemed to begin a cell phone conversation. He leaned back to reveal a tray on his lap, on which rested the biggest and best burger with fries you'd ever seen. Truly a disconnected sight, but to me, it looked like the Last Supper. I was like a vampire needing to feed, for I would die—the feeling of hunger was that intense. So I convinced myself of this: it was so hard having him sit there, I felt like a predator ready to pounce on his food and cell phone. He had no idea what danger he was in; the temptation was way beyond the night before, convinced the invitation was for only one drink and dinner.

Boy, did I screw up. I closed my eyes, began softly crying, and said a prayer to God; as soon as I opened my eyes, my gothic mystery man was gone, along with the burger and fries. I sat for a few more hours , completely miserable. I finally got up to go to the restroom, and then proceeded to catch my flight, only to see firsthand that   I looked as bad as I felt. By my reflection, I knew no one would loan me money or believe my story. I looked and smelled terrible, and to top it off, I had a big white zit on top of my nose. I was beyond humiliated.

I made it home finally, went through getting my card reactivated, promising myself I would never do this again. Several days later, I heard that small still voice of God saying, "I was in Houston with you. I knew you were hungry and thirsty. I know the whole story. I sent a man to help you, but you rejected him and Me—yes, your pride caused you not to eat or drink, and you had unlimited use of his phone. He was an honorable and respectable man. He did not judge you as you judged him."

I was mad that God would imply I had been judgmental.

"His heart was pure. Yours was not," God said calmly.

I don't understand.

"You're thinking right now, I'm referring to his demeanor and dress. Not so at all. He was transparent, you were not."

God was right (I know, an understatement). I was again ashamed of myself. I am sure, looking back on that occasion when he saw me hurting, that his spirit knew he needed to keep hanging out near me so I could be more transparent, more open-minded, and seek out his assistance. Heck, he might even have bought me my own burger, fries, and soft drink. But I couldn't approach him; I was close-minded and unfriendly.

I asked God why the man He sent to me said nothing.

"You would not have received it, Terry," God said. "The request had to come from you. It was in your heart, but you never allowed it to come to your lips."

I cried and cried; again, God was right, and I thought about how many times I had purposefully created barriers and used them to cut off people from what my heart was feeling because my lips couldn't speak it. How about you? Right now, at the office, is there something you're holding back? Do you open channels of communication or create obstructions to protect your own emotions?

CHALLENGES I OVERCAME

As I reflect on this noble learning experience gone wild, I am left with the very humbling realization that as much as I thought I was "all that" and a "wonderfully principled" professional, I was little more than a work in progress—and a bit sassy at that. Who was I fooling? Certainly not God. I didn't give in to the mad night of good-time partying. I joined in the fun and excitement and paid a price; you might say a few helpings of humble pie! If I take a wide-angle shot of the evening and morning, it's easy to see how my perfect little world was turned upside down by some of my own conflicting values and viewpoints. That heart/lips separation I mentioned earlier happens because of our perceptions, right or wrong, that others don't look like us, dress like us, drive vehicles like us, live in nice neighborhoods like us, shop like us, or believe like us.

The real challenge I faced in Houston was Terry—how in control or out of control I was. I believed God was with me, even orchestrating much of what was happening. Yet I was really disrespectful toward my relationship with my Creator... wasn't I? My main challenge was a test of my humility— something I view as a pure and authentic gift from God. When we open ourselves to *humility*, it almost feels like a magical whim and fantasy. However, I know of course God's no magician, though a tidy miracle worker!

The problem I had in Houston, as I look back reflectively, was with my lack of acceptance of God's gift of humility at its most basic form, that is, *a brand of non-ownership*. Do you see? I lost it. I missed it. I wasn't free to use humility at will and as abundantly as God provides because Terry got in the way.

Humility as *a brand of non-ownership* permits you to enjoy everything you own, or choose to encounter, or in which to engage, yet not obsess about owning it or protecting it. What a liberating concept!

25

Humility protects you from all sorts of unnecessary judgments, assumptions, and valuations of right or wrong usage.

Along the way (and I'm sure my mother influenced me), I learned it was not my job to judge or convict, but my job was to love. Houston was a reminder of how little I really understood that message!

I know I never want to be homeless (a spirit-sensitive experience) again, and I only want to receive

God's blessings in any way He sends them. I am hopeful and pray these blessings will foster our continued service on earth. And to my gothic dude in Houston, you made this story worth writing for many of us who must match what's in our hearts to what is spoken from our lips...or not spoken!

OVERCOMING YOUR OWN CHALLENGES

Okay, it's your opportunity to consider the tools I used to overcome my challenges, and consider how and if you can apply them to overcome challenges in your own life. You don't have to get stranded, as I was in Houston to feel out of sorts.

Suppose you walk into a new church you heard about from a coworker, which sounds like it might resonate with you far more than the church you've attended all your life with your parents. What challenges might you face as you try to follow your own heart? Consider the circumstances: the pastor has been there for twenty-five years, he baptized you, and counseled you through your serious break-up with your first steady boyfriend. Changing your place of worship can be an overwhelming experience; yet, remember, many life changes can be overcome with perspective.

Though that boyfriend quickly became history, the truth was, if I was honest with the results of the wide-angle shot of contradictions, it became apparent to me that my once-perfect little world was being mildly to violently turned upside down by some of my own conflicting values and viewpoints.

26

That heart/lips separation I mentioned earlier became powerfully more real as I had to admit my perceptions were right or wrong, not because their truth was right or wrong, but because I lost context, just like you might!

Put on your critical thinking cap: the one that truly recognizes other people don't look like you, dress as nicely as you do, drive a comparable vehicle, live in the right neighborhoods, or shop in the right markets. If it is the case, recognize your views may not be in line with others... and that's okay!

My huge challenge in Houston was how out of control I was while believing I was in control. Yes, I was intellectually in control, but I hadn't permitted my "spirit within" to fully connect with Our Creator—something that's the "essential let-go"— *that is, the spiritual and emotional state when you surrender who you are to who God is asking you to be or become!*

Essentially, accepting that God can believe in you (after all, you were His creation), but He will not orchestrate the orderly collision of energy and events necessary for you to achieve your dreams and aspirations. You must accept the free will God has given you to create the opportunities to achieve your dreams and aspirations.

A test of my humility, instead of it being a pure and authentic gift from God, as I look back reflectively, my lack of acceptance of God's gift of humility at its most basic form (*a brand of non-ownership*) was missed. I wasn't free to use the very humility God had abundantly provided.

YOUR TURN

- How many Houston-like memories do you have of how you didn't understand God's message?

- What blocked you from accepting God's humility?

27

- What are some examples of your non-ownership? Share examples.

APPLYING TRANSFORMATIONAL THINKING (TT) TO YOUR LIFE TODAY

Are you ready to put on your She Is All Business headset and give her the reins to take you to that place of Passion where God wants you to be?

- The people pleaser in you is conditioned to extend favor to receive recognition and a measure of favor in return. *Although we all have internal measures that urge us not to engage in unexpected behaviors, we are human and do stumble.*

- You can beat yourself up about it, but it's too late for that; however, it's often enough to recognize it and move on (intending, of course, not to compromise you again). You may recall, I fell for the "one client, one drink, my treat, that's it, I promise." All the while, my inner voice is screaming, "Don't get in," but my rebellious "out-of-state party girl and I can prove it" smiled   and jumped right in the limo with loud rock music playing. The price I paid was both an internal reflection on my weakness, insulting   my Father in Heaven, and almost missing a flight home from Texas to Nevada!

- *A transformational thinker* is resourceful, rational(?), yes, yet always resourceful, and focused on the resourceful solutions...or those that provide the needed provisions. When hungry, food is the required provision; *it is more important than your pride!* A military veteran acquaintance of my husband, Dr. John, panhandles a few days a month at the exact location to get enough money for his monthly rent—that is his essential provision —and Dr. John sees him monthly to contribute to this veteran's rental income! It is his way, his ticket to resourcefulness!

- Pay attention to those persons who present themselves to you in times of your need for provisions. As Dr. John is to the vet, *that gothic man in Houston was to me, but I rejected him, and ironically, my pride stepped in again to block me from God's provision!*

- Pay attention to humility's heavenly powers of magical whim and fantasy (not magical, but *transformational*), as your acceptance of God's gift of humility (*a brand of non-ownership*) permits you to enjoy everything you own, or choose to encounter, or in which to engage!

4

Hanging with the Monks in Big Sur

(Stepping out in forbidden territory, or a slice of heaven for this Pentecostal gal!)

THEMES

In my story, the discussions and examples that follow make references to these themes:

Surrender: Being a CEO of three companies, a mother who mentors her partner/ daughter in the businesses, a role model for so many other aspiring businesswomen and my staff, an industry leader, and a wife who stands by her dying husband was a lot of pressure; yet, God wanted me to surrender and spend some alone time with Him.

- *Silence*: Strangely moved to the Internet— totally out of character for me at that time…and the words I heard were silence and hermit—honestly! I searched for hermit/ silence and ended up at The New Camaldoli Hermitage in Big Sur, California.

- *Curiosity*: I warned them in an email that I was coming—a Pentecostal gal into a Catholic monastery —and they responded: All are welcome! After checking in and getting my room assignment, my nervousness changed to excitement and I was full of *curiosity*. I spent the remainder of the day exploring every bit of the grounds.

- *Prayer*: of course, I know Jesus Christ as my Lord and Personal Savior, and I regularly pray the Lord's Prayer. I'm sure my strong opinion of the Catholic belief system is not too unlike how Catholics might view my Christian belief system.

- *Supernatural*: the power and supernatural strength of prayer changes everything. If you never do it, then start today. *How? Just start talking to God, be humble before Him, and believe He will hear you and honor you.*

- *Listening*: the simple design for this place to hear God's voice was so easy: be quiet, watch your thoughts, focus on God's voice, leave the world behind, don't answer your thoughts with your thoughts. Just listen...you will hear, see, and experience God's presence. Such a presence came in many ways at this special gem tucked in the Big Sur Mountain Top.

MY STORY

Like every other Sunday morning, I was in my closet getting ready for church. Dr. John went down to the gym at our Country Club to get in an early weight workout. While looking through my jewelry, I heard God's still small voice say to me, "Terry, I need you to spend time alone with me." I paused at hearing this, but I knew it was God speaking to me. I didn't get His timing and found myself ticking off all sorts of excuses to explain why the timing was just so bad. The fact is, I tried to muster a strong defensive stance, but time and time again, my defense is never sufficient against God's offense. Silly, isn't it? We rationalize this and that with God, and yet He sees and knows all, and we still try to hide our emotions from Him and continue to make excuses for our indecision.

The truth is that at the time, I didn't want to have anything more placed on my schedule; business demands were enough to bear all alone. Add to it the needs of my company, employees, their families, Dr. John's narrow escape with death eight weeks earlier, and his current compromised health status were tugging at me. I'm not suggesting a comparison of character by any means, but I could only imagine what His disciples must have thought when Jesus commanded, "Follow Me..."

At that point in my life, I had little time for myself, and God was asking me to take time to be alone with Him. Looking back on my life at the time, a cell phone, iPad, and computer were my constant companions. Being a CEO of three companies, a mother who mentors her partner/daughter in the businesses, being a role model for so many other aspiring businesswomen and my staff, an industry leader, and a wife who stands by her dying husband was a lot of pressure...and God wanted me to surrender and spend some alone time with Him?

God knew best how much I needed Him that day. I always relied on Him, trusted Him, and drew on the personal strength and emotional fortitude He alone provided. But here I was, at this crossroads of sorts, running on empty when I thought my tank was full. My energy was deflated. I had mistaken nervous anxiety as adrenaline and ignored the stress and the weight of the pain in my life—in effect, I was badly coping with the mayhem in my life!

The nudging of His voice became curiously compelling: what did God really want me to do? What was my next move? I was familiar with speaking to God directly, yet He remained silent. I was strangely moved to the Internet, and the words I heard were silence and hermit—honestly! I searched hermit/

silence and ended up at the New Camaldoli Hermitage in Big Sur, California. Big Sur has long been celebrated for the unique number of havens it has nested over the past half-century. Still, it's not an inexpensive place to live, and access is quite limited. Still, this community is nestled in the coastal mountains and redwoods south of Monterey and Carmel. It's a place of spectacular ocean shoreline views, set amid naturally growing redwoods, oaks, madrones, and other native foliage along the Northern and Central California coast.

Amidst this beauty, every sort of artist, aesthetic, corporate guru, independent business owner, writer, author, health and New Age body/mind practitioner, body therapist, natural healer, massage therapist, and the like have lived in the beauty of the place we know as Big Sur for more than half a century. Yet, there on the computer screen in front of me was this Hermitage in Big Sur that I was being called to by God Himself. And after packing my small travel suitcase, I was on the road, some seven hours later, to arrive in Big Sur at the Hermitage. I was totally in uncharted territory!

Think of this: I was raised Pentecostal, and I was at a Roman Catholic Hermitage. What I knew of Catholicism came from the memories Dr. John shared with me of growing up Catholic, attending parochial schools all the way through high school, and his consideration of the priesthood. His second cousin was a personal secretary to the pope in Rome; however, he had left the Catholic Church when his mother died in 1970. All he wanted to do was sing a song he had written for his mother at her funeral, but at the time, the Church would not permit him to do so. So off Dr. John went to explore the broad world of religious fervor and indifference, including Buddhism, Hinduism, Judaism (his mother's mother was Jewish, and by law he was as well), and when he met me, Protestantism. He rarely talked about having been raised Catholic (that he could never sing his mother's song created a deep wound in him).

One of my close friends was Catholic, but she never asked me to attend her church. The only other person of Catholic

34

faith in my life was a coworker with whom I would talk about our churches and their differences. In fact, she told me about a silent retreat she once attended. It was not until many months later that I learned the very Hermitage I was headed to was the one where she had experienced her silent retreat. She, like so many on the Internet, never talked about her/their experiences, though I feel I must share what happened to me, because it could well happen to you, just like many of the other stories in my book!

Catholicism was like speaking a foreign language to me. I wasn't sure if I agreed with what I knew of Catholic beliefs. The words, songs, and expressions I had heard about in their churches were not at all inspirational to me. Yes, of course, I agree with the living presence of the Holy Trinity: God the Father, God the Son, and God the Holy Ghost. Of course, I know Jesus Christ as my Lord and Personal Savior, and I regularly pray the Lord's Prayer. I'm sure my strong opinion of the Catholic belief system is not too unlike how Catholics might view my Christian belief system, though I'm not sure of it.

What I could not shake was that God wanted me there in Big Sur; however, I've learned that when God talks, He means it. In simple terms, when God sets up an appointment for you, show up and be prepared for any...and...everything! Yes, it was perplexing and outrageous that God would call me on a Sunday morning to pack my bags and get down to Big Sur because He wanted to meet with me alone. What's more, driving to Big Sur required me to drive from Reno, Nevada, over a snow-covered Donner Summit, through Sacramento, several valleys, and past Monterey and Carmel before getting to the Hermitage. So, if I seem crazy to have done this, remember - there's a Bible story of God making a donkey talk to his master to take care of a vital communication issue!

I truly dropped out of my life for three days. Impossible for me to believe I could do this, since I had always been the foundation to so many life links for people in my life—responsible until I fell asleep exhausted each night. Similarly, how could I suddenly become unwebbed from my artificial connections to the world through my email and cell phone? Still, the thought was painful and seemed impossible, but hey, God was the chairman of the board!

I thought about all kinds of things, and it seemed like nothing as I moved from Nevada to California and through the inland valleys toward the California coast. Eventually, I hit Highway 1 and was cruising down the beautiful coastal highway south of Monterey. As I approached Big Sur, the ocean was on my right side with the mountain redwoods, oak, and madrone on my left. As I drove down this now two-lane coastal highway, my mind began wandering: did I really hear the voice of God? What was I doing here, and what was this really all about? In fact, it all seemed outrageous to a logically thinking mind. I wondered at one point: 'Did I miss the Hermitage altogether?' Maybe I got God's message mixed up. Remember, I had been driving for seven hours!

Pow! There in front of me was the sign my Internet directions told me I'd see. I slowed down to turn up the road and then realized it was a winding one-lane road that I'd have to travel for two miles before getting to the Hermitage. Off I was on what seemed like a four-wheeling adventure, but I was doing it in very low gear—and very slowly up a steep hill that seemed so high.

When I finally reached the end of the road, I had found the Hermitage. As I peered around, I had a most outstanding panoramic view of the Pacific Ocean. Wow! The ocean kept going and going and going into the distance, like a bird's eye view across the horizon of a vast ocean from a perspective I'd never known. The view was simply breathtaking, and as soon as I got out of my car, it was like I entered an entirely different ecosystem theretofore unknown to me. The flowers and plants seemed more vibrant and colorful than I had ever known, the smells were sweeter, and I noticed squirrels and critters were roaming around the grounds. It was an awe-inspiring moment to say the least!

Perhaps more potent than the captivating beauty of the grounds and environment was the silence and peacefulness that was hauntingly present. Imagine that for a moment – so much to see, experience, and appreciate; yet, an eerie silence envelops it with a feeling of very safe and comfortable peacefulness. My "spirit within" truly felt quiet and gentle. That sounded like a hint of heaven... Hmm?

When I arrived to check in at the Hermitage, I quickly learned that it was a place of *silence*; the only place you could talk to the monks was in the library/bookstore. Yes, they were classic-looking monks wearing long hooded robes. I warned them in an email that I was coming—a Pentecostal gal into a Catholic monastery —and they responded: All are welcome! After checking in and getting my room assignment, my nervousness changed to excitement and I was full of *curiosity*. I spent the remainder of the day exploring every bit of the grounds. I went first to the communal kitchen, where I encountered my first "silent" human and respectfully remained silent (not so easy for this gal). After, I walked a few of the paths around the Hermitage, checked out the inside of the chapel, and used my binoculars to spy on the area where the monks lived. I felt a little bit like Nancy Drew in disguise. I was beginning to allow myself to feel vulnerable and open...thus, receptive to change!

I had my iPad with me to take pictures, and as I walked about, I snapped all sorts of views and angles of the grounds. From my room, which was a very modest space for me, set away from the other rooms, I used different iPad camera settings to capture items of interest. At one point, I stood on the coffee table in my room to peer outside through the large picture window. I snapped a photo looking out the window, and in it was a graveyard.

Yes, my Hermitage room was almost touching the graveyard!

I took several other photos of the graveyard and left it at that, and as the bells rang for vespers, off I went to the chapel. I had no idea what I would be doing at vespers, but prayer had always been an essential part of my life. I was sure the monks had seen plenty of folks learn to adapt to their ways, and I'm sure they must have known the awkwardness many of us experience with our first vespers, but it was cool. In fact, it was more like Holy Big Sur because it wasn't vespers that moved me; instead, the presence of the Holy Spirit in the voice of God welcomed me to the place He called me. *And what's remarkable for me, as I reflect on the first vespers, is that the monks knew I was there at God's invitation, and that this Nevada gal wasn't their first rodeo.*

The vespers service was enriching, yet somber, and full of love. I could feel the warmth of God in this holy place, and it was clear to see the monk's love for God. I sat after the service, having wept and wept, thinking of how selfish I had been to God by not taking time (in years, mind you) to be alone with Him truly. Back home, He got a morning and evening prayer, Bible readings on Sundays at church, and a thank you shout here and there, but I never spent time with Him in prayer like I was spending here.

Yes, I feel church becomes a holy place as God's presence is ushered in through prayer and worship, but what struck me about the Hermitage was that since my arrival, it had felt and continued to feel like a holy place! *This was truly a place of spiritual communion, in silence, with God—a very personal and intimate meeting of spirit and mind with my Creator, conceived with His invitation, received through my obedience in prayer.*

The simple design for this place to hear God's voice was so easy: be quiet, watch your thoughts, focus on God's voice, leave the world behind, and don't answer your thoughts with your own. *Just listen, you will hear, see, and experience God's presence.* Such a presence came in many ways at this special gem tucked in the Big Sur Mountain Top.

The Hermitage is holy ground, a slice of heaven here on earth designed for those times in our lives' journeys when we want such a closeness and intimacy with God that only our total surrender to God can yield.

I recall reading blogs from a guy who stayed at the Camaldoli Hermitage. He obviously did not get it after 24 hours, as he wrote that he was bored out of his mind. Really? I reflect now on the many notices and instructions left by the monks informing visitors about the experience before us.

This is not a place for you if you are not interested in reconnecting to God!

Yes, that blogging dude missed the point entirely. I was struck with a sense of incredulity: how do you get to the point of having an opportunity to sit quietly with God and say you are bored out of your mind? I admit right up front that the life of the Camaldoli monks is curious to me. As I read it, their lives are simply secluded, set apart, and principled. They wear hooded robes, pray, and work without ceasing, and live silent, humble lives. In my studies, I learned that there are fewer than 60 Camaldoli monks worldwide. *It is a way of life on the verge of extinction. While this profoundly disturbs me, I pray that this book keep the spirit and holiness of the Camaldoli monks alive now and in the hearts of us all.*

Spending three days in conversation with God, while on the hallowed grounds of the Hermitage, was framed with the inaudible yet constant prayers of the monks as I journeyed with them in my sojourn with God. While yet silent, there was such clarity, purpose, and direction to my time at the Hermitage, and a sense of knowing I left with, that there will always be times when these monks and others like them will be praying for us. Even though we are unknown to them, we are known to God, whose children they pray for without ceasing.

How ironic it is that sometimes we are too busy or too selfish to stop, listen, and pray with sincerity. We must protect this sacred way of life for all those who do this on our behalf. Few men and women grow up saying, "I want to be a monk, nun, priest, minister, gospel singer, or prayer warrior!" I am ashamed and disappointed by how we all assume, or loosely say, that we will say a prayer for those hurting, because it's the right thing to say for you or for the other person to hear. But the question is: How often do we pray for others?

In my local 'Terry world' over the years, *those who know me have called, emailed, texted, or otherwise asked me to pray for them.* I always pray for those who ask for prayer. Sometimes I ask if they want prayer right away, no matter where we are. If it's uncomfortable because of my vocal Pentecostal roots, we do it later. *What's most important is that the praying gets done!*

I know some think it's a waste to pray; it leaves me a bit incredulous *because prayer is talking to God—that is it!* Prayer is asking for assistance, *and then getting out of the way for His response.* **Your pride is removed, and the great mystery of faith and believing is manifest once again in your life in response to the sincerity of your prayer!**

Sometimes, when people hear my stories and I say God spoke to me, they are stunned; yet God does indeed speak to all of us in many ways—often, we don't listen!

I know the power of prayer changes everything. If you never do it, then start today. *How? Just start talking to God. Be humble before Him, and believe He will hear you and that He will honor you.*

After attending evening prayer, I was so full of peace, in a state of complete stillness. I had found myself encouraged by the monks to journal , and I did. I found it very therapeutic and relaxing. *I still wasn't sure why I was there, though I knew I kept my appointment with God, I was wonderfully excited about what God wanted to show me and say to me.* Journaling at first seemed a chore to me, but after I began to do it, I couldn't stop. I wrote every thought, experience, dream, and wish on paper. It was like I brought it all to life, and then I remember how important it is to write, set goals, and cast your vision—*you know, if it doesn't get written down on paper, it doesn't get done.*

It's a fantastic connection; even God said, "Write it down in Habakkuk 2:2–3": "Then the Lord answered me and said, 'Record the vision and inscribe it on tablets; that the one who reads it may run. '" For the vision is yet for the appointed time; it hastens toward the goal and it will not fail. Though it tarries, wait for it; for it will certainly come, it will not delay.'"

As the light outside grew dimmer, I remembered my curiosity about the graveyard's allure and my resolve to get as close to God as He would permit me at this Hermitage, to which He called me to be with Him. Of course, I'm thinking in my Nancy Drew kind of way, who isn't captivated and intrigued by touching a graveyard? Just as the thought sprang into my mind, I was on top of the coffee table in my room, praying my weight would not break the old '50s-style table. Gosh, how embarrassing would that have been to have to tell a monk I broke the coffee table , standing on it , looking for ghosts in the graveyard?

Sometimes, the little girl in me, regardless of my age, cannot be tamed—all common sense leaves. So, there I stood, looking out the window, convinced I had just seen a golden retriever on the opposite side I was perched. They already had a dog, so I snapped a picture of it several times and then jumped off the table and got ready for bed. I had not slept in a twin bed since I was a child. That fact alone brought back the little girl in me.

I was exhausted and fell asleep by 8:00, to be awoken by bells ringing at 5:00 in the morning. I could hardly believe I had fallen asleep before 8:00 in the evening, and equally astoundingly, that I was wide awake at 5:00 in the very early morning. Back home, I have to take medicine to turn off my jet-fueled mind around 11:00 p.m.. I wake at least twice during the night, struggle to get back to sleep, then get exhausted and wake up from the war to sleep and stay asleep. The Hermitage was the first time in years I slept deeply — *yes, truly rested!*

As I wrote in my journal about all the magnificent supernatural dreams I had, my deceased mother and my golden retriever, Sophia, visited me. I found myself also more joyful in the morning and lacking the very usual feeling of dread or anxiety that often accompanies my days back home.

The Hermitage was a whole different place for my soul and spirit to take the lead in my behavior, while my mind took a while to catch up with the rest of me. And catch up it had to do because it was soon time to get to the vigils, the Lord's essay, and *prayer* times. The only descriptors I'm left with for these moments were wonderfully *supernatural*; they had a mystical yet holy quality, because the presence of God felt so real.

Of course, we must move from the most familiar to the unknown, and it was hard not to bring my Pentecostal mind/spirit set into the equation. *I realized God was in every religion, and I was determined before the next chapel to do Catholicism for Dummies on the fast track.* The only way to do this was to go, see, and ask those questions that were frustrating me. I needed to quench my curiosity. I wondered if they'd be ready for all of my questions - I had so many, and as I reviewed the pictures I had taken from the tabletop, even more questions arose. I started making a list of questions, *and as I studied the pictures I had taken on my iPad a day earlier, I was stunned by what I had captured.* I stood there staring in disbelief at four distinct images in the pictures. There were (and are still today) two dogs sitting by a tree, but not in the exact location as the other two distinct figures, an angel and Christ's head and forward-looking face.

I was floored. I marched down to the monks in the library area where they could speak, pulled one aside, and showed him the picture on my iPad. He half-grinned at me and, without missing a beat, commented, "Yes, that is what we hope for you to experience." I'm thinking, like this is a common occurrence? I walked away in silence, still in disbelief. I wanted more answers: how come no one talks about this place?

I'm somewhat in turmoil but thoroughly spiritually charged. I've travelled to this secluded Catholic monastery at God's invitation to have these supernatural experiences and see these manifestations in pictures I snapped on my iPad. I was seeking answers to questions so I could explain them to others; who would believe me?

But as I would quickly learn, *it was the reality of my experiences with God that mattered,* and I had other direct encounters with God at the Hermitage. Four of these experiences were physical encounters, like when I felt my hair being stroked from behind (at first, it felt like someone was behind me , combing it out, and yes, I have long hair). It happened as I was coming out of the bathroom. The first time, I spun around and was ready to kick someone's butt, and in an instant, the fight/flight response was replaced with a receptive appreciation.

The three times thereafter, I closed my eyes and received the heavenly touch, which felt loving and peaceful. One of these times, I felt goose bumps on my skin and had the sense it was an angel wanting me to reconnect with God. *I believe the Lord knew I needed a touch at the time, and I know the touch was real—a touch I felt physically and a touch I have not felt since.*

The next morning, I left the Hermitage after morning's prayer. I asked the monks to pray for me. They did that in the morning, along with their world projects. I felt incredibly sad when I left the Hermitage. I had just spent three days with God and the monks, and I had to go home and explain what God did in Big Sur! While driving, my mind wandered to that place of incredulity: *Who is going to believe me? It all seems so ridiculous—why me?*

I asked God again, "Why me? You called me to be alone with you and you placed me in the loving hands of your monks in Big Sur. It was not to have me return home to be humiliated. That can't be..."

I got my answer, as God spoke plainly again: "Who better than you?"

Okay, God, I'm no slow starter once I commit, so I've shared our relationship and the message of the New Camaldoli Hermitage in Big Sur, California. I will tell my story, share the supernatural pictures You permitted my iPad to take, telling people as you have said to me that the images you showed me through the camera were the only way they could be seen, *as to the visible eye, your glory and power are of such intensity that our natural viewing spectrum could not distill the light into concrete images.*

Indeed, what I had captured on my iPad is a pathway to the supernatural—*God's gifts peek through the shadows and light reflections that our naked eyes cannot handle!*

Postscript: December 5, 2013: Since I visited the New Camaldoli Hermitage in Big Sur, California, I have seen a few more glimpses of the spiritual world in pictures I've taken, reflecting on the camera and shadows I was shown in Big Sur while here in Nevada. God speaks of angels, and I have taken photos of angels assigned variably to persons in my sphere of influence. Some friends and colleagues who see the pictures argue over their gender identity and biblical theology. Still, I know my angel is female, and I believe Billy Graham's book, Angels, offers an excellent theological understanding of how you, too, may glance about your life and see your own angel! (Angel Picture Dec 2013)

CHALLENGES I OVERCAME

Often, our most significant challenge is something so very close to us that we'd never consider it a challenge—that is, until we interrupt it or are in a situation where we must cease relying on it as part of our normalcy or routine. Such was my challenge on three fronts, but in essence, these were but one: no cell phone (I live on my cell phone and everyone who knows me is aware of it), no iPad connected to the Internet (the other contact point people on which people rely on for getting in touch with me), and no talking... period (I'm a talker, I mean, talker...I mean, *talker*). I know, no big deal, but it was a big deal for me and drilled right into and through my comfort and discomfort zones and then right into the heart of my "insanity" zone.

Overcoming the "quiet zones" challenge was made easy by the environmental forces around me—that is, the monks, the Hermitage, others in residence, and plenty of what we kindly call peer pressure. *Kindly, yes, because peer pressure is really one of the tools you can use to help you overcome your own challenges.* The difference between using peer pressure to help you overcome challenges and feeling pressured by peers or the environment to behave in specific ways is in knowing who is interpreting and applying the peer pressure!

Your freedom lies in your full use of the elements of the environment around you, including the social and intrapersonal cues of the people around you, as well as the implicit or explicit peer pressures arising from the small group or social setting you're in. There's power in them thar' wills...people will telecast so much of what they want and need from you...if you listen!

What was especially valuable about my stay at the Hermitage in Big Sur is that I learned to listen with those faculties of mine that were always so preoccupied with the

45

ringtones on my cell phone, the message alert on my iPad, and the quick tongue otherwise stuck between my teeth.

OVERCOMING YOUR OWN CHALLENGES

How would you describe your routine day? Coffee in bed in the morning while checking emails on your iPad, notebook, or whatever, a shower, getting dressed, have breakfast, and then go to work. Or perhaps you take time to exercise before showering, get dressed, eat breakfast as you run errands, and then go to work. Get my drift: we all have specific routines we follow, not because they're law, but because they're comfortable, fairly predictable, and have the characteristic of something my Dr. John husband calls a stressless routine— meaning, we can pretty much get 'er done yawning.

Our friend, Kellie, seemed like the perfect model of stressless routine...until today. In effect, Kellie's perfectly organized world fell completely apart when she awoke and noticed a lump on one side of her neck. Instinctively, she righted her out-of-balance state of mind by reasoning that the lump was something muscular from the way she had slept on her new pillow. That was good for a day, but after another night's sleep, she awoke the next day with a lump on the other side of her neck—she now had lumps on both sides of her neck! Her stress-free routine was over… at least for now. As it turned out, weeks later, after testing, Kellie was diagnosed with lung cancer, and these two lymph gland reactions were her body's cry for help.

Again, your most significant challenge may be something very close to you that you'd never consider a challenge. Suddenly, you are forced to accept the reality of limitations — to your world, your freedom of expression, and your way of living — caused by a disease or injury you once ignored or denied. Maybe it is a mole on your body that's changing colors, texture, and shape, an infection that won't respond to treatment, or chronic abdominal cramping. I'll tell you, I'm not particularly a fan of peer pressure when its effect is to lead you around by the nose and render you a rather pointless follower with little personal initiative, but I don't mind pressure from my friends and loved ones for me to stop being stubborn about these kinds of potential medical issues.

My message is without hesitation: Take back your authority to overcome your challenges! In the following "Your Turn" exercise, let's explore how you dealt with change and how you viewed its effect on your life.

YOUR TURN

When was the last time you challenged yourself to change a portion of your daily routine completely—and what was the change?

FROM _____

and TO _____

- What were the most personally demanding elements of the change you experienced?

- What were the most personally beneficial elements of the change you experienced?

- Who else benefited from the elements of your change and how?

APPLYING TRANSFORMATIONAL THINKING (TT) TO YOUR LIFE TODAY

Transformational thinkers who know God's voice, listen for it, and know we are all most challenged and potentially open to God's voice **at times of emotional upheaval** in our own lives, or at times of **anomie** *(i.e., a lack of social and moral rights and wrongs – chaos!).*

If you do not hear from God audibly or internally, He may direct your actions as His form of communication—follow His lead; ultimately, doing so led me to Three God Communication Conclusions, gleaned from my time at the New Camaldoli Hermitage in Big Sur, California:

1. When God sets up an appointment for you, show up and be prepared for any and everything! I'm glad I had my iPad (and of course, He knew I would). Any coincidence that God called a Pentecostal woman to a Roman Catholic Hermitage, knowing her husband grew up Catholic, attending parochial schools all the way through high school, and almost went into the priesthood? God is *always* communicating to *transformational thinkers!*

2. Try this on with your **TT communication wardrobe** *(of techniques and tools to understand and interact with TT cues and opportunities)*: the presence of the Holy Spirit echoes the voice of God; getting to know the sounds of the Holy Spirit fine-tunes your ability to know with certainty God's intentions for your life. It's ***transformational to listen, to hear, to see, and to experience God's presence in your life!***

3. And be sure to include this in your *TT communication wardrobe*: **Know with certainty that people will telecast so much of what they want and need from you**...*if you listen with the God-given abilities you possess!* Use your listening to take back your authority, and remember that listening includes the social and intrapersonal cues transmitted by the people around you, as well as the implicit or explicit peer pressures

exerted on you by the small groups or social settings you're in throughout your life.

5

Loving the Source of Pain and

Suffering

(And letting go, because yet again, God's already made up His Mind)

In my story, the discussions and examples that follow make references to these themes:

- Disbelief: I was to leave the room, but I hesitated, frozen in time—they were whispering, but it was clear as a bell: "She's a baby herself. I'm glad it's up to you to tell her, I don't know if I could. Her son is very ill and is going to die." *These words made no sense; the only emotion I could accept was disbelief.*

- Love: I remember feeling hopeless and helpless, but Brandon was no accident - I loved him and would continue to love him as my flesh and blood. He was conceived and grew in me over all those months, and I would spend every bit of life I could with him.

- Let's be candid: you never overcome the pain of your child's death, but you learn not to be afraid of talking about it, and grow comfortable using your story and understanding of everything associated with it to assist others in understanding theirs.

MY STORY

This will be the most painful story I will tell in my life; I can't imagine anything worse, yet I know there are sad, defeating stories in all of our lives, stories that bring us to the brink of our sanity, and some that take us off into the abyss, a place I almost went at one point in this story. *Have you ever been there?*

All I can remember since I was a little girl is that when I grew up, I would get to be a mommy and be the best mom, loving my child like my mom loved us. That day came true when I found out I was pregnant with my first child at the young age of twenty-one. I was awash with the joy of impending motherhood, and I can remember the jubilance I felt. I felt excitement about becoming a mother, loving and nurturing my child, watching them grow, and all of it under God's watchful eye! This brought great anticipation and hope to our extended families. I just knew I would be the best mom a child could have, as I had been there for years alongside my older brother's children (my nephews) as they grew up.

My pregnancy was uneventful: swelling, getting fat, unusual cravings, doctor's visits, pregnancy checks, and more doctor's visits; yet, I loved every moment of it. My son was born two weeks early, weighing almost nine pounds. He was born perfectly healthy, my fulfillment—a firstborn male child; what more could I have asked for to start my perfect family life?

However, all that changed when I took Brandon to his first four-week check-up. I remember the day like it was yesterday, although it was thirty-three years ago. That morning, my aunt and my mother accompanied me to the doctor's office so we could all go out to lunch afterward and then get in some shopping. Such mornings were great examples of what I envisioned the next phase of my life to be.

What was to be a relatively regular routine check-up was dragging on. The pediatrician appeared to be spending a great deal of time with Brandon while he was lying on the examining table. I watched as he slammed his palm over and over again on the bed next to Brandon's head and little body. He was performing a Moro reflex test on my little boy, hoping to see an otherwise normal reflex response. Brandon had none, and the absence of the Moro reflex in an infant is abnormal.

The doctor left the room abruptly, leaving me there alone with a nurse and my baby boy. The doctor returned with a team of colleagues. Being a new mother, I had no other frame of reference but to wonder what was going on. I was conditioned to fairly routine visits, but it was clear that Brandon was the issue, and the nurse in the room said nothing. I had a passing thought that my mom and aunt might be getting hungry.

I suppose it was instinct, but I began to study the faces of the doctors in the room intensely, and their expressions were not what you might expect from a joyous viewing of a new baby boy. In fact, their expressions did indeed suggest something was terribly wrong. I was confused. This was my cute, bubbly baby boy. They were staring back and forth at my beautiful gift from God. Suddenly, their conversation stopped, and my doctor asked me if I had come alone. I told him my mother and aunt were with me, and with that, he suggested I get them and bring them into the room—that the doctors had something they needed to tell me. It would be better if my family were with me.

They turned their backs to me as I was about to leave the room, but I hesitated, frozen in time—they were whispering, but it was clear as a bell: "She's a baby herself; I'm glad it's up to you to tell her, I don't know if I could. Her son is very ill and is going to die." *These words made no sense; the only emotion I could accept was disbelief.*

I slowly opened the door; my heart had been pierced with a javelin. I approached my mother and aunt in tears, crying hysterically. The stinging in my eyes from my tears is as real a feeling today as it was 35 years ago. With mascara running down my face and into my eyes, I was blinded, seeing only black. I raced to my mother's arms, my heart pounding so loudly it was as if it was in my ears. I was panting, my legs were weak, and I felt like I was going to collapse from the weight of my *disbelief that had become despair.* It took only a glance from my mother and my aunt to ignite a bloodcurdling scream from me before a waiting room full of young mothers and their mothers: "My God, why? What went wrong?" I yelled. I then collapsed in my mother's arms, sobbing uncontrollably, mumbling repeatedly, "Mom, they said Brandon was very sick and is dying."

Both my mother and aunt marched into the examining room like women on the front line, going into a battle they knew they would not like. I stood in the hallway staring at the door, thinking that maybe there was a way to avoid crossing the threshold to what was inevitable pain—that if I remained standing right there, I could return to the perfect little family I had created around my son, Brandon.

I could hear my mother, the warrior she was, talking to the doctors and demanding answers to the flurry of questions she was firing at them like bullets leaving a gun. I remember feeling hopeless and helpless, but Brandon was no accident, and I loved him and would continue to love him as my flesh and blood. He was conceived in and grew in me over all those months, and I would spend every bit of life I could with him.

Ours was a *love* with no boundaries. I knew only to love Brandon, and I did so for his eight months of life. No one knew what it would be like. Doctors couldn't really tell me how I would react to loving a child whose reality would be a maze of clinic visits and hospital stays, specialist testing, doctors' visits, and travelling to many different cities and out of state. Was our focus to truly understand what we were supposed to do to help Brandon enjoy the life he had? *I wondered at times if I wanted more to find out why God let this happen: why would He give me a child to love, nurture, and raise, only to snatch him then away?*

October 4, 1982, is a day that will be etched in my memory along with eight months of sorrow and devastation. I will remember this day forever because this is the day I witnessed the small white casket, which encased my one and only child, descend into the earth through a dark hole. My arms ached. No longer would they hold and comfort him; instead, the walls of God's earth would embrace and comfort him forevermore.

Sadly, I turned away from the painful sight. My body felt numb; I didn't understand. "Why," I wondered, "why me?" I couldn't stop asking. While I knew Brandon died and had been buried, it was difficult to accept he was really gone! Even as I walked to the car that day, ugly thoughts invaded my mind, which had fast become a battlefield. I imagined that as soon as we all turned away, he might wake and be smothered, and I wondered, "What if he gets cold?" I tried to veto these hideous thoughts as soon as they stormed my mind, but I was slowly losing the war. *I was consumed by exhaustion, and my entire body could no longer oppose the repulsive enemy. Satan had taken advantage of both my emotional weakness and youthful age to render me obedient to his lies and distractions.*

Emotionally broken, my body drifted into sleep, while my soul retreated to its private sanctuary in the arms and presence of God—a place of spiritual strength and certainty where Satan had no authority, influence, or power.

It was a long and grueling journey home. My *disbelief* often gave way to the jolt of reality that I was going home without my son. When I arrived home, my thoughts turned to how I would disassemble his baby room. My home seemed like an empty shell through which waves of memories cascaded off its walls. I rationalized with myself: *If I keep the door shut to his bedroom, the thoughts would all go away.* But I knew I couldn't; I had to deal with it. Slowly, I unlocked the door to his bedroom. Suddenly, I felt a surge of emotions sweep throughout my body, engulfing me with great sorrow. I collapsed to the floor, clutching his favorite toy to my breasts, and wept, knowing this would be the final time I would see this room as *his room.*

As time passed, I regained control of myself and began the once-dreaded task of neatly packing his belongings. Some friends asked me if packing up his room in any way felt like I was burying him all over again. Honestly, I had already said goodbye, and while I thought it would be a lifetime before I could ever forget Brandon, my work right then was really a matter of concealing the material reminders of his eight months of life.

Brandon's horrific suffering cannot be explained well. Still, his disease, Werdnig-Hoffmann (the severest form of muscular dystrophy, which strikes infants between birth and six months old), while rare, is well understood. *Death was a waiting game, yet the time in between his birth and death was a loving game.* My little angel strained to make sounds as he had no muscle control of his larynx or lungs. There weren't any high fives, tickle sessions, or crawling trips on the floor. *The day Brandon died, he died in my arms, gasping for his last breath and in pain; there is no other pain like this.* At that moment, a part of me died forever, *and when he was buried, part of me entered the cold earth with him to be with him forever.*

When I look back, I remember all the sadness and hurt—yes, but I also remember all the people who prayed for Brandon and for me. I remember how strong my mother was throughout the eight months and the years thereafter. So many people really tried to lift me spiritually and emotionally. While I know and appreciate all of them, I know that, in the blink of an eye, today, thirty-three years later, I can crash into tears. *The difference in the tears today is that, while they are tears reflective of a sad time, they are also tears that celebrate my love for Brandon... and motherhood... and life... and God!*

Every year at Brandon's birthday, I wish him Happy Birthday, and each year, the day of his death passes, sometimes quickly, sometimes with more of a lingering memory. There wasn't complete solace in Alfred Lord Tennyson's expression: "'Tis better to have *loved* and lost than never to have *loved* at all." I've wondered many times in my life why God allowed this to happen. Sometimes, there is no apparent answer, yet with living and loving, these challenging moments bring insights to light. God had already made up His mind about Brandon, and my lesson in the throes of the pain was ever evolving... even to this day. *What is it to love without boundaries?* Do others I love deserve the same? How about others you love?

CHALLENGES I OVERCAME

There were many days over the years I truly believed I had overcome the pain of Brandon's death. *Now I believe you never overcome the death of a child you bore through delivery, birth, and infancy;* instead, you learn to understand aspects of the meaning of that life: (1) how specifically Brandon's life had meaning to me, (2) how Brandon's life shaped me emotionally, (3) how Brandon's death grieved me, but opened me to God's voice and a rebirth of my motherhood, (4) how Brandon's death gave me an authentic heartfelt (not intellectually reasoned) understanding and appreciation of life beyond birth, and interestingly for me (5) how Brandon's death crystallized my opposition to abortion.

Somehow, this kid of twenty-one developed a sincere and richer appreciation for parents who know their children may be born handicapped, yet draw on the strength of God's provision to bear the child and allow them to learn life as a child of God. As mind-blowing as it might seem to many would-be and young parents, there's a love that's not easy to explain unless you've faced the challenge and felt the love so few parents ever really know, having born a child with a fatal genetic disease or disabling life condition.

OVERCOMING YOUR OWN CHALLENGES

As you've read, I've included this "Overcoming Your Own Challenges" section to help you consider some of the tools I used to overcome my challenges as tools for overcoming your own challenges in life. Still, there's no magical, mystically conceived, or spiritually profound formula I can give you for overcoming the challenge of the death of a child.

As I write this, I realize I've just shared a horribly depressing stage of my life as a young Christian mother who never expected anything like what happened, to happen... especially to me, based on my relationship with God. Now, thirty-three years later, that very relationship with God has truly fueled me and prepared me to write with vigor, because in sharing my story, I genuinely appreciate how Brandon still lives in me and through me. My love for him and what this love brings to my passion to write this book for you, the reader, and for me, the mother, is real indeed!

Let's be candid: you never overcome the pain of your child's death, but you learn not to be afraid of talking about it and grow comfortable using your story and understanding of everything associated with it to assist others in understanding theirs. Implicitly, you do not have to be a licensed psychologist, therapist, or ordained minister to share your experiences of losing a child or a loved one. You are the expert at that if you have lost a child.

I encourage you to review or revisit your experiences of the loss of loved ones and identify how they impacted you as a survivor, and identify as well how you think others can learn from your loss or glean some understanding of their own loss

58

from what you're willing to share openly and honestly, free of guilt or shame about your loss. While your loss may have been decades ago, sharing your experiences, seasoned by time, will be insightful and help others understand their losses from their own vantage point of *faith or belief.*

My Christian advice: Listen to God's Holy Spirit and share from your heart; release your inspired reflections to others. If they're right on, others will know exactly how to use them!

YOUR TURN

- Have you experienced the death of your child?

- How old were you? How old was your child? Tell us about what happened.

- Is there a message you would like to share with other parents about your child's death, your reaction, and how you're doing today (today's date)?

APPLYING TRANSFORMATIONAL THINKING (TT) TO YOUR LIFE TODAY

Are you ready to face the realities of your life's past to launch you into your future transformed, having learned and grown from these life experiences? Open yourself to that place of passion where God wants you to be!

- Painful memories are real, be they recent or nearly a lifetime ago, when the memory itself is of a life lost from a life born unto you; *living is not about getting over losing your child of less than a year of age to a tragic genetic disorder.* Living is about recognizing and grieving the loss, *then overcoming the paralysis of that loss to fulfill the purposes of your life!*

- *Transformational loving* is loving without boundaries; given the situation in your own life, yes, you can love a baby who you know is dying but is not yet dead—with all your heart, soul, body, and mind—*for you will always find joy and honor in knowing, remembering, and loving this child of God!*

- *Transformational loving* may as well be conceived of as the A game you play between birth and the certainty of infant death from a genetic disease.

- And if *transformational loving* is indeed loving without boundaries, do you qualify as a *transformational lover* to those you love in your life, *and are you a willing recipient of transformational love* from others? If not, it might be worth clarifying your love boundaries!

6

My First Encounter in Hearing God's

Voice: A Miracle Was Breathed!

In my story, the discussions and examples that follow make references to these themes:

- Craziness: Living a life of craziness! My thoughts and emotions were all over the place. Craziness happens when you must bury your one and only son. Craziness is realizing you will never see him grow up, screw up, and make up—that you will never share his milestones that every mother dreams of for her child.

- Bible: It was now Christmas Eve, and I pulled out my King James Bible that my mother had given me "to read and keep close to my heart." She told me without hesitation, "It is not a book, Sis, but God's Word speaking directly to your heart."

- God Talk: I wasn't sure I wanted anything to do with the expectation of God-talk, but then—*pow*—I felt an unexplained, compelling urge to open the Bible. Again, it was Christmas Eve, and like robots, I guess, we had a Christmas tree with lights on it. At this moment, the Christmas tree lights were the only ones on, and as I opened the Bible, they began flickering.

- Unthinkable: Several doctors and geneticists from the University of California, Davis, wanted to interview Steve and me because Brandon's disease (Werdnig-Hoffmann) was so rare. Steve and I agreed and met the doctors several days later. The conversation with specialists began as a relatively routine question-and-answer session—or so I thought. Family health history questions, our health histories, their impressions, and then the unthinkable! *These so-called experts proceeded to inform us that if we had any more children, they most likely would die as Brandon had.*

- Listening: I sat across the small conference table from them, listening to their horrific and unthinkable babble. I informed them that I was already eight weeks pregnant. Without missing a beat, and as a matter of fact, their response was to say almost in two-part harmony, "Then you should have an abortion." I had just buried my son, and yes, I knew it was raw. Still, I had yet to tell anyone I was again pregnant. I was still shy to say to people, "God said this child He gave me will be perfect."

MY STORY

After burying my son, Brandon, in October of 1982, I fought many bouts of crying spells, depression, and suicidal thoughts. I didn't disclose the full story of Brandon's funeral. I couldn't; it was too harsh. I so believed God was going to bring Brandon   back to life. I lifted his tiny body out of his coffin and brought him close to my chest, fully expecting him to come alive. Onlookers and family thought I was out of my mind; perhaps, but my faith was so strong that I held on to the belief that my baby boy would respond to me. He did not; in fact, when I attempted to look into his eyes, the eyelids were sewn shut, as was his mouth , to my fingers probing to get inside. I was an emotional catastrophe capable only of imploding. I had nothing left.

I took Brandon in my arms and ran out of the funeral parlor; I couldn't surrender him at that moment. Stronger minds and wills prevailed, and I surrendered my boy and finally accepted the reality of October 4, 1982, a day etched in my memory along with eight months of sorrow and devastation. The day I witnessed the small white casket in which Brandon was again placed and in which he would descend into a dark hole in the earth will not be forgotten. My arms would no longer hold and comfort him...never again in this lifetime.

Returning home, it was so difficult to look at his empty room; it was even more challenging to see other women with children or watch my sisters-in-law yell at my nephews and say the kids were driving them crazy. "Crazy"— that word was so loosely tossed out of their mouths. I wanted to say, "Come into my mind. I am living a life of craziness!"

My thoughts and emotions were all over the place. Craziness happens when you must bury your one and only son. Craziness is realizing you will never see him grow up, screw up, and make up— that you will never share his milestones that every mother dreams of for her child. I would have given anything to have a living son to drive me crazy!

I never thought my life would go on without him. The days became months, and this dark cloud of confusion and doubt hung over my head: my son died of a genetic disease, leading to more doubt, depression, and sadness, as now, my hopes of motherhood seemed to be dashed, all but impossible.

63

In the early 1980s, there was no practical way for testing, let alone screening for this dreaded disease. My family and friends seemed disconnected; no one knew how to help me.

I had lost considerable weight because eating had become a chore. I remember days when I wouldn't shower or eat much more than a few pieces of bread. I got to the point where I was ready to give up; I didn't even want to maintain the space I was taking up on the planet. I was a messed-up *mess*!

Over the next couple of months, I ebbed and flowed, sad to okay, but was never really happy. It was now Christmas Eve, and I pulled out my King James Bible that my mother had given me "to read and keep close to my heart." She told me without hesitation, "It is not a book, Sis, but God's Word speaking directly to your heart." Honestly, I rarely understood much of God except for fire and brimstone teaching/preaching. I feared God and had been taught a lot about how He would get you if you sin, but I was taught very little about a loving God who is full of grace!

I realized at the oddest of times, even then with the Bible in my hands, that I was blaming myself for Brandon's death, that I surely did something to deserve him dying. I frankly did not want anything to do with God or any consideration of God talking to me through His Word in the Bible. It all seemed so impossibly supernatural, mystical, and magical, and none of this healed my hurt over losing my son to a genetic disease. As I saw it, my life had been full of tragedy, emptiness, and pain— why could I possibly believe in some magical and mystical fantasy with God? I looked at my mother's life at the time as well and thought *she loved this God and prayed and went to church, and her life was yet filled with sadness over my father's behavior.*

How could I believe this same God my mother loved, even as she suffered, would ever want to talk with me... or to me? I wasn't sure I wanted to have anything to do with the expectation of God-talk, but then - pow - I felt an unexplained and compelling urge to open the Bible. Again, it was Christmas Eve, and like robots, I guess, we had a Christmas tree with lights on it. At this moment, the Christmas tree lights were the only lights on, and as I opened the Bible, the lights began flickering.

I closed the Bible immediately and said aloud to God, "God, You took my son—why would You do that? What have I done for You to punish me?" To this day, I can still remember the directness of my words to God and the anger and confusion in my voice. Yet as I spoke those words in rage, God's Holy Spirit was speaking to me: "Isaiah 49:20, Isaiah 49:20..." As I suggested earlier, I knew little about the Bible except for the children's stories we all grew up hearing at Sunday school and often learning to recite: Adam and Eve, Noah's Ark, Jesus's birth, John the Baptist baptizing Jesus, the death and resurrection of Jesus, etc. Even though part of these stories were from the Old Testament, I really had no sense of the Old Testament, so why *Isaiah 49:20,* was I making this up?

As I stared at the now-flickering Christmas lights, I wondered how *Isaiah 49:20* came into my mind. As if my mother had instructed me, I grabbed the Bible and started fumbling through it to find the *Book of Isaiah* and then the *forty-ninth chapter and twentieth verse.* Finally, my finger on it, I read it slowly: *The children which thou shalt have, after thou hast lost the other, shall say again in thine ears, The place is too strait for me: give place to me that I may dwell.*

I was in disbelief. I must have read it twenty times until it began to sink in and take root in my spirit. It was the most profound experience that ever happened to me! I slowly started to see life differently. I had real hope and belief that I would have another child. God told me so; it was right in His Word, word for word! I was in awe.

My mom was right: God did talk to me, and He spoke to me with the most important words I needed to hear. As I basked in the moment of a newly found peace (I was sure I'd never feel again), I marveled at the awesomeness of God. I cried happy tears and would swear today I heard God's voice speaking to me: "I understand how you feel, My child, I also

65

lost My Son." I believe God wanted me to know that my anger was okay; that He understood it and the pain I felt. And that night, He promised me another baby and a healthy child. My covenant with God was sealed, and now I could confidently step out in faith, standing on Isaiah 49:20 and my encounter with God. I would be sustained through all the naysayers, doubters, wrecking crews, and even among all those who loved me most.

In January of 1983, I told my husband Steve that the Lord was nudging me to step out in faith, and that meant no birth control. Steve, a believer as well, was confident, based on how I told the story, that I really had an encounter with God! He saw a profound change in me that few could recognize as accurate; he agreed I had changed overnight! Of course, as time would prove, convincing Steve was the easy part. Exactly to the day he stopped using birth control, I conceived and was again pregnant. In retrospect, remembering the joy and excitement I felt over the pregnancy could have only been there because God had blessed the pregnancy. I knew I was going to have a perfect child given to me directly from God! I knew the pregnancy would be ideal, full of love, excitement, and anticipation…as it turned out, though, from only Steve's and my eyes.

Brandon's death was still fresh on everyone's minds. Grieving was less than four months old, and yes, I missed Brandon terribly, but God removed the painful grief from my heart. He knew I was going to need supernatural strength to carry this pregnancy to term, and he wanted this baby to be a happy, joyful baby—and she was!

I was already two months pregnant, although no one else knew, and I received a telephone call from my local pediatrician. He asked if I would mind meeting with him in the next couple of days. Several doctors and geneticists from the University of California, Davis, wanted to interview Steve and me because Brandon's disease (Werdnig-Hoffmann) was so rare. Steve and I agreed and met the doctors several days later. The conversation with specialists began as a routine question-and-answer session—or so I thought. Family health history questions, our health histories, their impressions, and then the *unthinkable! These so-called experts proceeded to inform us that if we had any more children, they most likely would die as Brandon had.*

They went on to discuss in detail how we passed on the gene to create this dreadful disease, again, one of the most severe forms of muscular dystrophy; we were reminded that no child has ever survived it. With any new pregnancy, we had a 25 percent chance of passing on the same mutant gene to our baby—*in effect, handing our baby a death sentence!* Their advice and the overall discussion turned bleak.

As professionals in their fields of study, their advice was not to risk having any more children on our own, but possibly to adopt. I sat across the small conference table from them , listening to their horrific and unthinkable babble. *I informed them that I was already eight weeks pregnant. Without missing a beat, and as a matter of fact, their response was to say almost in two-part harmony, "Then you should have an abortion."* I had just buried my son, and yes, I knew it was raw. Still, I had yet to tell anyone I was again pregnant. I was still shy to say to people, "God said this child He gave me will be perfect."

Everyone in the world would have thought I lost my mind. However, because I was so mad and knew this to be true, I stood up and told them just that! And just as I thought, they sat there in complete shock. I don't think either of them took a breath the whole time I told them the story. I had to carry this baby in my body. God knew I would need to have my full armor on. The bullets were just beginning. *I stood firm in my faith and never wavered.* That was so difficult for so many to understand. I waited until I started showing at five months to reveal I was pregnant again. For my family, it wasn't a moment of joy, but of my mother busting out and crying uncontrollably and saying over and over again, "Sis, please tell me you are lying." My church family was in absolute disbelief.

I wasn't sure what to make of the negative gossip-mongering chatter I was hearing about my being a martyr or just a crazy young woman desperate to have a child, no matter what. It got to be an echo, "She deserves whatever happens…" Not one person in my family, church, or any of my friends believed me or supported my pregnancy, except my husband, Steve. When the news spread that I was again pregnant, people treated me like I had a contagious disease– that anyone who talked to me or came near me would catch it!

Over the four or so months remaining, I had a perfect pregnancy. I ate whatever I craved, among my favorites, tuna and watermelon. I swam, walked, read, and frequently thanked God. Yes, I was grateful for His promise and for His love in speaking to me that night so many months ago. Do you know what it feels like to know God has your back… unconditionally?

Sarah was born one day before my birthday, on September 14, 1983; ironically, the day a year earlier, the doctors told me Brandon was dying and had to be hospitalized. Brandon was born two weeks early and weighed 8 pounds, 9 ounces. Sarah was born four weeks early, but weighed almost eight pounds.

Sarah, my God-promised child, was born perfect.

CHALLENGES I OVERCAME

The doctors in the delivery room leave, and I hear them talking and asking if my first child was the one with Werdnig-Hoffmann disease. Ironically, even at this most celebrative moment, they were still following me—the challenge I had to overcome was a medical community that doubted that I knew what I was doing, and a psychiatric community that thought I was a martyr.

Her daddy named her Sarah Elayne, princess of light. When I took her for her first visit to the same pediatrician I had taken Brandon to see, he said to me, "I know you told everyone about your child, that God spoke to you about her; well, she is beautiful!" He then said, "I want to know your God!"

Thirty-five years later, Sarah and I are business partners and the Broker Co-Owners of Reno/Tahoe Realty Group, LLC, our real estate company! Ah, but she's way more than that: she's intelligent, a high school honors graduate, a college graduate, an athlete, a musician, an artist, a beautiful Hispanic woman, a philanthropist, and a co-founder and board member of the Dreams Foundation, Inc. Sarah is married, has a toddler son who is the love of Dr. John and my lives. Reflecting on Sarah's life, it's clear that God gave her extra doses of love, compassion, and caring for those in need. She does know her story, and she does know she has the genes of a warrior! *And yes, she does have the gift of hearing God talking to her.*

If I had aborted her as the doctors suggested, I would have been left empty, and worse, I would have dishonored God. And frankly, had this been the case, I could have very well committed suicide while high on drugs. The challenge I had to overcome was fully believing in and trusting that God had indeed spoken to me about Sarah; she was to be my blessed child, and I was never to doubt God's word and to enjoy the pregnancy and get ready to be a mommy for a very long time, and now into my future to be a grandmother to my legacy who will live on, I believe, to achieve greatness in his contributions to communities and organizations who serve persons in need of spiritual encouragement.

The overwhelming message I carry forward to others: don't listen to people; exercise listening to God's voice!

OVERCOMING YOUR OWN CHALLENGES

Okay, let's be blunt: Has anyone ever told you that you were crazy? Perhaps in the derogatory, when you're called a martyr, dismissed as stupid, or just tagged as plain nuts?

Yeah, that went with the territory concerning Sarah, but I had the strength of belief in God's Word to overcome all of it. But let's venture down the trail together; I know I didn't always have that assurance, nor may you.

There's no mistaking that I have a track record of faith and trust in God, along with plenty of stumbles and missteps. So, when we face any challenge, it might be wise to try to at least generally classify where that challenge fits in our own encyclopedia of challenges. This isn't an Einstein request, but only that you break down your challenges into manageable bites. As challenges relate to this chapter's theme, they have everything to do with *trust and confidence.*

In effect, we're talking about overcoming challenges where you are relying on only your own judgment or instinct about whether you can trust another person to get something done. What must you know about the person to place this trust in them? That's the question you must answer, and only time and experience will teach you what you need to know to trust another person. *Once* you've established these parameters of trust, you're free to exercise this *trust.*

The question of *confidence* in another person *comes entirely from you imputing to the person* your belief that *they are fully capable of accomplishing a task, activity, function, etc., on your behalf or at your request.* Your strategy should be simple: work only with people in whom you have confidence!

Looking back on my pregnancy with Sarah, I had essentially an entire medical community that was pretty sure I had no idea what I was doing, nor knew or understood the risks to my newborn, and a psychiatric community that essentially tagged me a foolish twenty-one-year-old martyr out to prove a point.

YOUR TURN

- How many times have you specifically heard God's voice directing you to do or say something you felt to be entirely plausible and possible, yet that others found inconceivable or crazy?

- What blocked you from acting on God's voice?

- What are some examples of people's advice you've taken that turned out to be disastrous?

- How about people's advice you've taken that turned out to be fantastic?

- Do you see any differences between the two types of advice?

APPLYING TRANSFORMATIONAL THINKING (TT) TO YOUR LIFE TODAY

Get ready to get your She Is All Business headset on, and give yourself the reins to take you to that place of Passion where God wants you to be!

- There will be moments you'll say and do the unthinkable and preposterous—your strength as a *transformational thinker* is recognizing these moments may appear to come out of nowhere or be triggered by horrific events ,   in response to which your thoughts and emotions explode all over the place. These crazy moments for *transformational thinkers* are, as Dr. John says, go-with-the-flow moments and not to be viewed as moments of dysfunction. That's a mouthful, but I know he's right!

- Occasionally, you need to recall moments of faith, belief, or trust so profound that recalling them today, right now, enlivens your spirit of *transformational thinking and living* as a change that's integrated in body, mind, heart, and spirit.

- Occasionally, you need to recall moments of faith when you have known that God has unconditionally had your back...As I do from time to time when I think of my God-promised child, Sarah, being born perfect, less than a year after I buried my son, Brandon.

- Want to really hang it out there and live a transformational life? Don't listen to people; exercise listening to God's voice! *He wants us to hear the transformational truths He has in store for us!* I'll say it once more: in my pregnancy with Sarah, an entire medical community was sure I had no idea what I was doing, nor knew or understood the risks to my newborn, and a psychiatric community that essentially tagged me a foolish twenty-one-year-old martyr out to prove a point. My point: obedience to and trust in God!

7

Your Mom, My Mom

(Teacher, confidant, friend, critic, role model of patience, long-suffering, God-loving generosity, and a voice I still hear, listen for, and value!)

THEMES

- Perseverance: The story of my mother meeting President Bush is nothing short of unbelievable; some who've heard me tell the story call it heroic, like the stuff of great movies. I see it as "daughter love" at the highest, but even more, I view it as a supreme example of the power of perseverance.

- Endurance: I could go on and on with stories of my mother's life after becoming disabled, stories that make you wonder from whom she drew such strength, grit, and endurance. You needed to be around her for only a short while to know that her praise for God and her daily communication with Jesus were as much a part of her life as the water she drank from her special non-spill water bottle throughout the day.

- Friendship: The staff was like part of our extended family for all those years, and they loved my

73

mom as thoroughly as professionally appropriate. We were permitted to decorate her room so that the essential things in her life surrounded Mother. As God's plan would have it, the staff that cared for her from the start was there throughout her five-year stay.

- Sacrifice: And most certainly, having a sense of the essential personal sacrifice that may have been required of us ensured we raised the bar of our commitment to mother so she could be certain our commitment was irrevocable.

- Love: The facility permitted my mother to have a pet as long as we provided for its daily care, feeding, and potty needs. Maintaining its necessary shots and/or medication as required was part of the deal as well. And as if led by God, we got her a young, mature cat she named Tiger Joe, who quickly became her companion, truly, the love of her life, and her leading man!

MY STORY

We all know our mothers in one way or another, and we all have some good one-liners to describe our moms that have likely changed over the years. But before I get into the punch line story of this chapter, it's essential that you really understand the state of my mother's health and life.

My mother, long divorced from my father, lived alone, freely and relatively independently in Carson City, Nevada, in one of the four homes she owned. She, too, *loved* the Lord and served as my Christian role model since my youth. Dr. John and I often took my mom to church with us on Sundays, either by herself or with her gentleman friends. Mom was very social, well-liked, and generous to her family, children, friends, and community. She was fun-loving, had the nickname "Hillbilly Grandma" from her roots in Tennessee and the Hollers of Virginia, yet was an impeccable dresser and really the life of the party.

As I sit here typing, a symbol of something gone very wrong sits alongside the keyboard. It's a handmade three-inch-diameter ceramic bowl with handles on each side, about an inch and a half deep. It's something that's held my special jewelry for a dozen years since a most fateful day in March of 2003.

Dr. John and I were packing our house in the middle of our move to Reno, about twenty-five miles from Carson City. My mom had been house hunting with us to find just the right home where we could all live together—a two-homes-in-one kind of property, and praise the Lord, we found the perfect place with horse property to boot for my mother's horse—yes, her horse!

That fateful Saturday afternoon, I received a call from my mom's gentleman friend, who had invited her to lunch at a local Carson City Casino, after picking her up from her weekly hairdresser appointment. They had never eaten at this casino; it was a new adventure for them, yet what I would hear on the phone call that afternoon would be a life-changer! My mom and I were best friends; we dressed alike, talked alike, traveled everywhere together; she was everything to me, my best friend.

The call revealed that, as my mom and companion were walking across the valet parking lane to enter the restaurant, the valet driver pulled away to park a large Denali SUV, then stopped unexpectedly and backed up hurriedly. *As he did, my mother was struck and thrown in the air like an egg being flipped in a frying pan, landing twenty feet away from where she was hit!* The call was numbing, and within literally minutes, we were on our way to the hospital emergency room in Carson City to be by her side. She was lying on the table in the emergency room and in excruciating pain, screaming and crying out Sis (my nickname), "Sis, Sis, help me!" She was truly in agonizing pain, yet to the visible eye, she looked perfectly groomed, only her hair a little messed up and some dirt smudges on her clothing.

Looks can be deceiving —obviously—as she squirmed back and forth on the table, crying and screaming about something very horrible that none of us could see. I remember immediately calling our pastor. I couldn't figure out why more wasn't happening faster. I looked around to find her friend , who had invited her to lunch, and he had gotten up and left. I was stunned. I knew his injuries were minor scratches, but he left my mom lying there, writhing in pain; where in the heck did he go?

I found the doctor and begged him to give her something for her pain. He looked at me like I was crazy; as I said, from the perspective of her lying on the table, my mom looked quite well. It seemed like hours before the hospital staff realized the crisis at hand. They gave her test after test with no medication, and I had grown increasingly impatient and demanded they do something— she was still aching and crying in pain. Finally, a physician ordered a CAT scan, and what he discovered was shocking!

My mother's liver was lacerated; she was full of blood and essentially bleeding to death! Compounding the problem, my mother was at the time taking blood-thinning medication for other medical reasons, so the hemorrhaging was essentially out of control. In 2003, the local hospital in which she lay did not have the level of trauma care needed to treat the injury. The Regional Trauma Center , thirty miles to the north, had the appropriate equipment and available surgical staff to save my mother's life. As she was transported to the hospital, we drove to meet her there for testing and treatment.

I remember her lying on the table in excruciating pain, crying and begging for relief. The trauma doctor on duty said the prognosis was simply that she was dying, and there was little they could do to save her life. *Of course, we knew of another physician's skills and prayed mightily that He intervene!* I cried next to her and with her and told the doctors to do whatever they could to save her.

Five days later, in the ICU at the regional trauma center, mega doses of blood-clotting drugs were coursing through her veins and internal organs, and the bleeding had stopped; however, her life would never be the same, ever again! During the bleeding, clotting, and trauma of the accident, she had a severe stroke, and the next twelve months of her life were spent in rehabilitation hospitals and at-home rehabilitation therapy. Mom had every type of rehabilitative therapy available—speech, physical, occupational—to relearn how to walk, to talk, chew, use a fork and spoon, take a drink out of a cup, use the toilet, groom herself, essentially everything one needs to survive and get along in the world. While she regained some measure of success with some of these, she never fully recovered. For the next eight years of her life, she needed assistance with almost every daily function.

With perseverance, she learned to walk, maneuver, and acquire other adaptive skills, and, owing to her tenacity, she lived with us for two years in the Reno house we had all intended to live in together. Unfortunately, repeated strokes and deterioration physically and logistically defeated the best of our plans. Our next housing search as a team of three was to find the very best assisted living facility that would meet our mother's social and lifestyle needs, while affording her safe living and access to friends and social activities.

Mother beat all the odds the doctors had given her after the accident, and her perseverance became the basis of her endurance as she lived out her remaining seven years in assisted living. Wonderfully, the last five years of her life, we had been able to place her in a lovely facility connected to her hospital, just a few blocks from our business office and fifteen minutes from our home.

The staff were like part of our extended family for all those years, and they loved my mom as thoroughly as was professionally appropriate. We were permitted to decorate her room so that the essential things in Mother's life surrounded her. As God's plan would have it, the staff that cared for her from the start was there throughout her five-year stay.

Right from the start, the facility permitted my mother to have a pet. The story of Tiger Joe and Dr. John has been told by many – all with the same punch line: those two really loved my mother, each in their own way, each one every day with little exception.

Dr. John never missed a day over the five years (unless he was out of town on business) of visiting my mother's assisted living facility to make sure Tiger Joe had food, water, his litter box was cleaned out, and he got out for a bit of walkabout while Mom was in an activity or otherwise out of her room.

Little is more accurate than the statement that "pets are good medicine," that they are vitally important to the disabled and elderly for companionship. Tiger Joe loved our mother unconditionally. He lay all day, cuddled up on her legs, neck, or asleep next to her on her pillow. He always made sure she could see him somewhere close to her. And not so surprisingly, if Tiger Joe or Momma needed anything at all, Dr. John and I were only a phone call away.

Understand, my mother was essentially bound to a wheelchair at this point in her life. Every week, she had her hair done by a professional outside the facility and sometimes in the facility as well. Every Friday, we hired a caregiver to take her shopping so she could spend her money buying things she enjoyed or to purchase and give as gifts to her friends and family. Every Saturday, she would go out with us to the movies, to eat, to "bargain shop" the thrift stores (one of her favorite treasure-hunting activities), or to go on an adventure or two! We felt it was so important to maintain her routine because it was something she could count on, think about, and plan for!

It is so crucial for people at any age, and especially the elderly who lose their independence, to have a routine upon which to create certainty. Safety nets are imperative via telephone conversations, reassurance, and just plain old-fashioned human contact. It was the saving grace for all of us that Mom saw us and interacted with us daily, as we did with her.

Regardless of her hardship and limitations, she celebrated life and people to the fullest. Whomever came into Christine's world, loved her "hillbilly, take no prisoners" attitude, and her seemingly broad array of nicknames and "Yearyisms" (her maiden name) or her just plain "Chrissy says" this or that…, and most certainly, knowing the importance of the personal sacrifice that was required of us, ensured we raised the bar of our commitment to mother so she could be certain our commitment was irrevocable.

She was herself unique in every way; she deeply loved the Lord and believed she could do just about anything. She was the Master of "wishcraft": *if she could not herself get something she wanted, she would figure out a way for someone to get it for her, or to do something for her!* Nothing surprised me when I got a call from the facility, like: "Terry, your mother is with a man in bed…"

"And your point," I'd respond, "she is entitled to express her love!"

"Terry, your mother insisted I help her open a charge account at XYZ store and asked me to sign the application for her, so she could get the clothes, purses, hats, and shoes she wanted", so says one of her caregivers after returning from Friday shopping. Or how about another caregiver who said, "Terry, your mother had me take her to a drug paraphernalia shop so she could get a secret can in which she could keep extra prescription drugs of her choice." Or how about this one: "Terry, your mother made me get her a marijuana capsule so her pain would go away." Or a call from staff at the facility: "Terry, you need to get down here. Your mother slapped another person for making fun of her and calling her a name."

And finally, a fitting example of how spontaneous a shopper my mother could be, given the setting during the

Christmas season. Always on the lookout for something unique and what she considered a must-have item, we were strolling through Macy's one Saturday. Unbeknownst to either Dr. John or me, Mother had reached up as we passed a display of these lizard-looking purses, snatched one, and thrown it into the shopping basket we had attached to her wheelchair. We had already bought her the gifts she wanted, and we were a little surprised when we got to the cashier's line and the purse appeared.

"I just have to have it!" she insisted. "But, Mom..."

"Sis, I want the purse—it's perfect. I must have it." "But, Mom, you have so many purses..."

That was it; she persisted like a little child who wanted a new must-have toy or doll, and when I said no, she began screaming, "Help, help ya ya ya ya ya." It was like her adult tantrum.

Dr. John and I were like, "Okay, we understand," but we were horrified to say the least by the stares coming from all directions, seemingly directed at us, like we were doing something terrible to Mother. We told her she was creating a scene and needed to stop. "Okay, Sis, just get me the purse and I'll stop." I told her that if she didn't stop, we would leave the store. She was still for the time being, and I glanced at her to make sure she understood. Surprisingly, she gave me a big smile and, moments later, began singing aloud, "Feliz Navidad. Feliz Navidad..." You guessed it—she got the lizard purse.

Yes, like you, I could go on and on with stories of my mother's life after becoming disabled, stories that make you wonder from whom she drew such strength, grit, and endurance. You only needed to be around her for a short while to know that her praise for God and her daily communication with Jesus were as much a part of her life as the water she drank from her special non-spill water bottle throughout the day! Yes, I have many precious stories of my mother's love, her kindness, her generosity, and her wittiness that I will cherish forever, and that will no doubt influence how I live and love in my later years.

Was it difficult and trying? How many times have you wiped your mother's bottom, bathed her, or washed her private parts? It was challenging at times, almost painful, but she has been gone since July 4, 2011. We have all the best memories of a truly remarkable lady who was Mother to me, Momma to Dr. John, Grammy Dorothy to my daughter Sarah, and a loving sister to her twin sister Maxine and older sister Beaulah—both to whom she mailed money monthly to assist them financially and to add comfort to their lives...even as she lost her ability to ambulate, enjoy her weekly shopping trips, and get out and socialize.

Before her accident, she read a lot. She loved children's books, the Bible, and most curiously, almost all of the "gossip papers" and popular magazines like the National Enquirer, Star, People, etc. After her accident, she had me and others read stories to her from these publications, and television became a significant source of her keeping up with what was going on in the world. It wasn't that my mother was a news junkie, but she watched and listened to a great deal of television news. She paid attention to stories, particularly about her political favorites, and President George W. Bush was one such favorite.

So one day, Mom phoned me *(we set up her phone for speed dial and got her a phone with extra-large numbers so it would be easy for her to reach us)* to tell me she had heard a news story that President Bush was coming to Reno, and she wanted to see him. As I mentioned, she listened to the news and enjoyed political debates and talk shows. Mom was vigilant and savvy; those who knew her understood, and others were often shocked to hear her strong political views.

So now, a once-in-a-lifetime experience with my mother, and given the state of her health and wheelchair-bound life at the time, please join me as I joyously relive with you my mother's and my improbable experience at President Bush's second-term campaign appearance in Reno, Nevada, when she shook George Bush Jr.'s hand.

Put simply, the story of my mother meeting President Bush is nothing short of unbelievable; some who've heard me tell the story call it heroic, the stuff of great movies. I see it as "daughter love" at the highest, but even more, I view it as a supreme example of the power of perseverance!

So, here's the setting: President Bush is speaking at a large outdoor setting in one of Reno's great park and recreation areas. Thousands of people have tickets to the event, and it is packed full. My brother, Danny, and his wife, Karen, are together with my mother and me. Mom was in her wheelchair, and much of the outdoor area was grass and packed-dirt pathways, with paved parking lots.

The stage where President Bush was speaking was well away from the parking lot, and it was quite a walk to reach the staging area. Danny helped me push Mom across the traverse, but the crowds grew thicker as we approached the staging area. When I tried to push my mom up into the handicapped area, the people just swallowed us up ,   and we literally morphed into and became part of the throng. *At this point, Danny and Karen were history; it was just Mom and me alone in the crowd.*

When we finally made our way through the thousands of attendees, we ended up about ten rows from the stage in an area reserved for persons with disabilities. *Like many public arena disability set-aside areas these days, the occupants seemed mighty handy and hearty, but hey, just more incentive for us to be creative.* My mother was so excited to be seeing President Bush, yet clearly disappointed that she really couldn't see much at all with the people clamoring around us and towering over her as she sat nervously in her wheelchair. *The opportunity to see President Bush in person brought a spark of joy to her life.* Yet the reality of the crowds brought tears to her eyes, as her fondest hope had little chance of coming true. Her life had enough pain and sorrow in it. *Okay, that was enough; it was time to suck it up, take additional risks, and overcome the odds.* Something snapped inside me, right then and there; in that very moment, I knew intuitively that I could do more. It was just me and my mom, *and when we put our minds and hearts together, it netted wonderful moments!*

"Hang on, Mom," I said, as I grabbed her arms and threw them around my neck to pull her up and out of her wheelchair. "We're going to meet President Bush!"

That said, I turned my body around, my mom's arms still around my neck, so my already failing, disabled back faced my mother's front. I bent over at the waist and hoisted my mother onto my back and told her to *hold on and never let go! I then started plowing my way through rows nine, then eight, and so forth, as close as we could get to the stage. She clung to me like her life depended on it.* The wheelchair was left alone and abandoned in the crowd.

You're correct: I couldn't see a darn thing very clearly, but I had good directional movement. *Interesting how people just got out of the way of this unusual sight moving through what was little different than a mosh pit of concert years gone by:* a strong daughter bent over carrying her mother on her back in a sort of turtle-like configuration ,   trying to get   to President Bush, uttering nothing but "Excuse me, excuse me." I was a moving force powered by something within that flowed from my love for my mother and my deep desire that her dream of meeting President Bush be realized.

I told my mom that, as we got closer to the stage, she should be prepared to let go of my neck if she had a chance to reach out to the President. We couldn't get all the way to the stage, and I prayed that God would find favor for my mother.

Please understand, the obvious was not acceptable - we had tried so hard and I had given my all to make my mother's dreams come to full fruition. Then the unexpected, nearly inconceivable, event happened right before us. *With my mother atop my back, her outstretched arm caught the President's eye.* Truth be known, his Secret Service officers weren't too thrilled with what the President did next. The President leaned and reached from the stage stairway enough to grab my mother's hand. Not only did he hold it, but the President also shook my mother's hand, then put his hand on her forearm and said these three words: "God bless you!"

The rest of the afternoon was a flurry of excitement for Mother. She told everyone who would listen— and made those who wouldn't—about her meeting President Bush, their handshake, and his asking God to bless her!

CHALLENGES I OVERCAME

There's absolutely no question that the single greatest challenge I overcame with my mother was my mother. Once her mind was made up, she was the proverbial pedal-to-the-metal lady. Her desire was so great and authentic that anything less than giving it my all for her sake wouldn't cut it. And the good news for me was that Dr. John was right there to support the craziest of stunts.

Mom's wishes translated our challenges in advance; we often knew what we would be up against, it was just that we weren't sure how taxing the situations might get. Like going street dancing with her, we would be on our feet, she in her wheelchair, rocking along with the music. Similarly, a trip through an outdoor zoo, an environmental park, or into gold and silver mines with her in her wheelchair all required unique adjustments and planning.

Once we agreed, any of these varied excursions were reasonable and could be safely accommodated. The execution and overcoming of the challenges happened by knowing and believing they were valuable to Mother's sense of value and worth! My biggest challenge was indeed surrendering to her perceptions of what was important to her from week to week…and why. The reality surrounding getting the things she wanted to do, buy, or mail, the places to which she wanted to travel, experience, or even live, and finally the specific piece of clothing, purse ,   or piece of jewelry she wanted...almost all had to be accomplished within the framework of Dr. John's and my schedules.

For the most part, we broke down the major elements of these requests. We lumped them together into our "Momma Needs and Wants Planning Checklist", and from here on out, it was far easier to stay objective and task out the many activities. Right? Of course not, but at least we began to recognize the need to plan, so family members, Mother's caregivers, and others who dropped in and out of her life would know when excursions or outings were scheduled. The "calendar" would serve as the source document for all of us... including mother!

The planning checklist was routine, and given that cost was never an issue, the issues were really more or less logistical in nature: (1) how many chaperones are needed, (2) what type of vehicle is needed, (3) what's the time frame and will medications be needed, (4) what kind of physical accommodations may be needed to be taken. Based on the answers to the above questions, several adjustments were made. For example, suppose Dr. John needed   to   take Momma to a doctor's visit or to an off-site laboratory. In that case, he could almost always do this himself. In some weeks, there could be as many as three to four of these visits, and his favorite ride was his hiked-up Jeep Wrangler 2-Door. When he drove the Jeep instead of taking the Mercedes, he had to carry a special red step stool he made for Momma to use to get in and out of the Jeep with his assistance.

He referred to the little red stool as one of his two Momma accommodations!

Similarly, if Momma was going to come up to our house for lunch or dinner during or after appointments, Dr. John had made a special green ramp we could set at the base of the two steps to the front door landing and designed it such that it was a smooth incline from the pavers' walkway in the courtyard, up and over the two steps to the front door and into our house: Momma's other accommodation. Thus, Mother's wheelchair entrances   and   exits were smooth, without jolting her spine, which was an area of medical vulnerability. *You see, the whole point of planning things like stepping stools and ramps was not to cast them with immediacy in mind, but with the longevity of Momma's health in mind.* This is a basic ingredient of planning checklists or frameworks that others can follow, or from which you can model the construction of your own!

We took this planning seriously when it came to travelling across the state line to California's San Francisco Bay Area (not such a big deal). Still, we took it to the nth degree when we planned a trip to Tennessee so my mother could see part of her family for what would probably be the last time. Planning was essential: airline tickets, seating arrangements, a 38-foot-long RV upon our arrival in Nashville, and a carefully laid-out itinerary to give her a trip she'd never forget. In addition to seeing the family and spending time with all the Yeary clan, my mother asked to go to Dollywood, an adventure retold many times over the months that followed.

Such great memories, enhanced two years later when Sarah, John, and I took my mother to Disney World. When it came to planning, we had this trip covered from every angle, even hiring Fairy Godmothers (a business enterprise) to help with my mother's care and grooming during the journey, so our time together as a family was focused on fun and leisure. Although my mother was in a wheelchair, we spent five days in Disney World together, in ways transcending the disability with laughter, silliness, Mickey Mouse ears, and fairy godmothers.

OVERCOMING YOUR OWN CHALLENGES

What I learned most and intend to share in this section regarding challenges that arise from already *complicated sources* (hold on a moment for examples of these *sources*) is that you need communication strategies, allies, planning checklists, to-do lists, and patience to pull it off if you're also a *working girl!*

To kick this off, let's look at four not-so-uncommon examples of what I referred to as complicated sources: (1) a disabled mother or family member who relies on you for overall life management; (2) extended family and parental in-laws in need of your physical, social, emotional or financial assistance; (3) a business you own, operate, or manage; (4) the breadth of civic and business commitments you make as a productive member of your local civic and national professional business communities.

Think about #1: obviously, there are books written about caring for your loved ones, and my intention here is to cut to the chase scene on some of the essentials that cannot go unmentioned. Depending on the severity of the disability, what's your *communication strategy* for dealing with a parent or family member who has lost the ability to maintain personal hygiene? This topic must be addressed candidly and immediately, including who is responsible for bathing, maintaining cleanliness, and, yes, even grooming Mom or Dad's private areas. Certainly, here's an area where personal care attendants may be enlisted, along with other grooming assistance; nevertheless, if Mom or Dad is living with you, it's an area of adaptation you'll need to make. Failure to do so, while *exercising patience*, frustrates the very essence of the caring relationship.

Think about #2: extended family and in-laws' parents who need your physical, social, emotional, or financial assistance. Talk about getting humbled! Think about it: you're running a multi-million-dollar business, and your disabled brother, Mark, who's on Social Security Disability says quite candidly and innocently to you, "Krystal, I'd like you to send my brother Bobby about $50 by the middle of every month so he'll have extra money for Burger King and McDonald's—he loves their burgers and fries." Yes, you do his checkbook for him, and there's no way he can send Bobby $50 and have enough money for his own necessities. You've got many options:

- Tell Mark he doesn't have the money to do this and discourage him.

- Compliment Mark on his concern for his kid brother and suggest he send a more modest amount, maybe $10–15.

- Sit down with Mark and carefully go over his budget and explain his financial limitations, asking if he wants to sacrifice anything on his own so he'll have extra money to give Bobby—working together to arrive at a dollar number that seems reasonable.

- Or why should Mark need to leverage his life and emotions for $50 a month? And even though there's a decade between you, isn't Bobby your kid brother as well?

Think about #3: owning, operating, or managing a business, particularly your own, is likely the backbone of your development as a resourceful, self-thinking entrepreneurial woman, yet you certainly benefit from having a silent source of power lingering about you and may well be the very family members for whom you are providing comfort and care. I realize that many of my most outstanding achievements in business occurred while I was deeply involved in caring for my mother. *Many of my breakthrough moments were met with applause from my mother, who was indeed rooting for and cheering me on every step of the way.*

When we reflect on those days, we will long remember the plethora of communication strategies, allies, planning checklists, to-do lists, and sheer patience we needed to manage our world of owning and managing Reno/Tahoe Realty Group, LLC, and providing my mother, the proverbial pedal-to-the-metal lady, with an authentic life. And yes, the good news for me was that Dr. John was right there for

Momma, Tiger Joe, and for me—to support the craziest of stunts I came up with.

Think about #4: I hear people say the same thing all the time in response to the breadth of civic and business commitments. We must invest in being productive members of our local civic and national professional business communities. I admire the commitment made by Madeleine Pickens, whose 501(c)(3) organization, *Saving America's Mustangs* (SAM), raised the necessary millions to develop and open the Mustang Monument Eco-Resort and Preserve in Northeastern Nevada. expresses powerful influence and a history of the   same: not only did she save over   600 mustangs from slaughter, during the disaster caused by Hurricane Katrina in August 2005, she organized emergency aid for the multitude of homeless animals in New Orleans, and arranged and paid for aircraft to evacuate over 800 dogs and cats to many Southern California shelters and humane societies.

Indeed, let's take our appropriate roles in our civic and business communities. I'm proud to mention that, along with my husband, Dr. John, and daughter, Sarah, we're very excited about the progress of our 501(c)(3) Dreams Foundation, Inc., a small public charity, which we founded in 2011. Our licensed Nevada Nonprofit Corporation has sponsored fundraising events at ArrowCreek Country Club and supported several programs for Veterans (e.g., free bus and taxi passes, Adopt-a-Vet Dental Program, home ownership assistance, and sponsored the purchase of Veterans' guitars); American Cancer Society Dinners, MS Society Walkathons, CARE Chest of Northern Nevada, a community dining program for senior citizens in a Reno area Mobile Home Park, a girls' softball team, faith-based organizations, an adolescent boys' treatment center, a home ownership assistance program for low-income single parent families, Solace Tree for grieving families, the Children's Cancer Foundation, the Humane Society, Veteran's Companion Dog Programs, a $50,000 donation to our community hospital NICU, local and regional community food gardens, a Reno area women and children center, and a scholarship program for a graduate student in business committed to working in the field of human services. Our family, along with our realtors at Reno/Tahoe Realty Group, LLC, and the Dreams Foundation, Inc., have supported a variety of human services programs.

The challenge before you is this: Will you be successful enough to be a productive member of your local civic and national professional business communities? How much you will be able to accomplish for and in your local civic and national professional business communities!

YOUR TURN

Have you ever found yourself in the situation of being called upon to care for any of the following:

- Your sick or injured child who was temporarily disabled for three or more months;

- Your ill or injured spouse is temporarily disabled for three or more months;

- Your ill or wounded parent is temporarily disabled for three or more months;

- a sick or injured parent-in-law temporarily disabled for three or more months;

- A sick or injured relative is temporarily disabled for three or more months;

- Any of the above is permanently disabled.

Once you recognized the responsibilities inherent in your temporary or permanent caregiver role, how did it change the way you felt toward the person for whom you were caring?

And reflecting on that time today (or to your current situation), how do you view the need for backup help (in hospice, respite care is a form of backup or relief for primary caregivers to give them some time away from the demands of caregiving for a loved one), checklists, planned routines, order, and predictable daily schedules, etc.?

Did you have any experiences with brothers and sisters that paralleled my experiences with Mother, or were they completely the opposite, or somewhere in between? It would be good for all our website readers to know about your experiences; thank you!

Please help us to elevate the roles of Christian businesswomen in our civic and business communities by telling us and others what kinds of things you do as a Christian businesswoman in your civic and business communities.

APPLYING TRANSFORMATIONAL THINKING (TT) TO YOUR LIFE TODAY

Are you ready to put on your She Is All Business headset and give yourself the reins to take you to that place of passion where God wants you to be?

- Tell the stories of your mother's love, her kindness, her generosity, her wittiness— her traits that you will cherish forever, and that are likely reflected in who you are today. You are grounded in your genetic and behavioral heritage—*recognize it as a jumping-off point for a life of transformational living!*

- Tell stories that reveal your mother's character and the intimacy of the adventure you shared with her, because this reveals your transparency and the untapped areas

91

of transformational living you may be ready to share with others in your life. I will long remember the freedom I felt in knowing that when it was just me and my mom, and when we put our minds and hearts together, big things happened! Politics aside, it's cool to have been a part of President Bush himself leaning down from the stage stairway enough to be able to shake my mother's hand, then put his hand on her forearm and say, "God bless you!"

- Apply these two storytelling opportunities to your father or other loved ones who have left you inspired, motivated, and transformed by their words, mannerisms, and ways!

8

When Angels Visit!

- Angels: "There are angels all over the room; don't you see them, Sis? There is one right next to you. Do you feel his wing on you?" I couldn't feel a physical touch, but in my mom's newly alive eyes, I could see we were not alone, and I answered, "I can, Mom, I can!" A little smile came on her face; it may have been the last smile I would see on my mother's face. We know and believe angels regularly minister to people of the Lord; they did in biblical times, and there was no reason to doubt my mother would ever be excluded from such visitation.

- Visitation: We had learned from the tenth chapter of Job, twelfth verse, that God's visitation to Job had preserved his spirit, and we knew the visitation of angels my mother experienced was there for her safety, not for our observance or edification.

MY STORY

June 11, 2011, was my mother Christine's seventy-fifth birthday. It was also the day our golden retriever, Sophia, died of a massive stroke in front of our eyes. Sophia had long been one of Momma's two golden retriever slobbering sweethearts; the other was Brandy, my four-legged niece. Less than a month later, my mother would be on her way to be with the Lord. *We had learned from the tenth chapter of Job, twelfth verse, that God's visitation to Job had preserved his spirit.* **We knew the angels who visited my mother were there for her safety**, not for our observance or edification.

My mother had one other close call with death in December 2009 when she was extremely ill. Doctors told us they were sure the pneumonia she had developed would take her life if her body weren't strong enough to combat it. Two significant things happened at that point: we prayed, I mean, prayed (!), and we believed in the doctors' and nurses' ability to respond to the situation. Mother was eventually stabilized and survived the pneumonia, and because she did, she became eligible and qualified for us to have her enrolled in a private Medicare-certified and state-licensed home and community-based hospice program.

This program permitted her specially assigned hospice nurse to visit her in the assisted living facility where she resided, and permitted specially assigned hospice homemaking aides to see her as well, to provide bathing and additional personal care services for the remaining eighteen months of her life.

Hospice had evolved well beyond the old model of palliative care for terminally ill persons with a six-month or less life sentence from the end stages of chronic and some acute diseases or conditions. We knew the palliative care hospice model well from my husband, Dr. John, a psychologist and hospice staff trainer who, for six years, coached staff and families on his "Living with Dying" care model.

Indeed, this updated and more family-inclusive model of home and community-based hospice program of care afforded palliative care (i.e., pain management), social interaction and skill enrichment, spiritual/pastoral counseling and engagement, personal companions/caregivers, and some financial assistance that varied by household.

For us and my mother's benefit, the hospice staff and the assisted living staff worked in complement to each other to maximize the care and services my mother received. So, if there was an infection to fight, there was a united team to fight it, and if there was depression, both hospice and assisted living staff coordinated their care for Mother.

The battle was especially tough from the days following her birthday until her death twenty-three days later. *The intensity of care exceeded the capacity of her treatment team to manage. It required a commitment from me and Dr. John to be by her side and/or on call 24/7.* There were a few nights we had to race down the mountain to answer middle-of-the-night panic calls from care staff, but they were only precautionary calls. We knew by her birthday that her health was rapidly changing. That day, we received the news that we knew, but had dodged for years – she was going into congestive heart failure. Her knees began swelling, then her legs and feet. It became extremely difficult for her to ambulate, even with the assistance we had given her for years.

We all remember her birthday when we took her to her favorite restaurant for dinner! *She was always fashion-conscious and had a special new ensemble to wear for her seventy-fifth birthday— clothing, diamonds, jewelry...the works—no fooling!* She almost looked like a cross between Dolly Parton and Elizabeth Taylor. Her appearance was so important to her wherever she frequented; she always wanted to make sure her "glam" was on...yes, even at seventy-five!

My brother, Danny, Sarah's fiancé, Howie, and Dr. John carried my mother in her wheelchair to the car and later into the restaurant. We weren't going to let logistical barriers get in the way of our birthday dinner for Mother, nor dampen our spirits! My mother was all about fun; it'd be odd to see her sitting still at any outing or event. She was always on the go, celebrating life and everything in it. She always gave tremendously of herself in every situation. She had a knack for providing and encouraging others to feel special, but there was one minor character flaw in her DNA: *if she thought you had done wrong against her, you paid the price deeply!*

Mother had no problem going from point A to B in a nanosecond to set the record straight. Sometimes with her, this happened in public settings. I can assure you it was highly embarrassing for all in attendance. Still, afterward, she would go on with life as though nothing had happened. In the throes of the "event," her venomous words could be harrowing and hurtful...but at times required! The few of us who stood by her side and those who experienced the venomous bite became immune to it, but those who didn't understand this rarely, if ever, returned to her life.

Doctors, specialists, neurologists, and consulting psychiatrists all concluded she had suffered irreparable brain damage in reaction to the car accident. Her difficulty in healing from the physical and mental trauma triggered a series of post-accident strokes, which, in fact, showed that the brain damage was accumulating over the years. In plain language, the effects of the brain damage were getting worse.

We wanted her to be comfortable and surrounded by the things she loved. Dr. John was with her daily for hours at a time, watching TV, reading the Bible to her, listening to music, and singing to her. My office was literally three minutes away , so that I could drop in and out throughout the day, and Sarah was in the office with me and would bring over her shih tzu, Stallone, to love on mother.

SHE IS ALL BUSINESS

As we saw her life slowly slipping away, it was very sad. Yet, it was also a relief to know the increasing physical discomfort she was enduring was also coming to an end.

In a very odd way, the process was likened to a vast, vibrantly colored balloon with a tiny leak that, day after day, would lead to its deflation.

As Mother's spirit deflated each day, she began to experience crossovers to the spiritual side of life or death. *She would twinkle momentarily as she told us of dancing with angels and waking up from dreams, telling us she saw family members of hers who had already passed.* Listening to her speak of these experiences was like listening to her as a lucid, loving, content mother I so loved and was beginning to miss so terribly.

At one point, as she was lying in bed, she abruptly got fixated in front of her and to her side opposite where I was sitting next to her, and her eyes wandered about the room a bit. "Sis, Sis, do you see them?"

"See what, Mom?"

"There are angels all over the room. Don't you see them, Sis? There is one right next to you. Do you feel his wing on you?"

I couldn't feel a physical touch, but in my mom's newly alive eyes, I could see we were not alone, and I answered, "I can, Mom, I can!" A little smile came on her face; it may have been the last smile I would see on my mother's face. We know and believe angels regularly minister to people of the Lord; they did in biblical times, and there was no reason to doubt my mother would ever be excluded from such visitation.

In truth, we can only see spiritual things with the eyes of faith. If you don't believe there are angelic ministers in your life, you will never see them. Similarly, you cannot see the things of the spirit if you have unbelief.

Angels are integral to our walk with God and were always topics of discussion when Mother and I mused over the wonderfully powerful spiritual goings-on in her room. With a wink or two, or near the end with a squeezing of our fingers, we all had the presence of being able to feel the sense that there were indeed angels in our midst. Let me be clear, these were not angels we worshipped in any form or function—you know only demons might try to seduce you to get you to worship them as angels—as once you succumbed to such deception, they could well manipulate you.

Yes, there was something profoundly beautiful about that experience in her room, and her smile was a sweet sign-off from my most important spiritual mentor. It was as if scripture was speaking directly to my heart at that moment, right from the 91st Psalm, where we are told *God has given His angels charge of us, to guard us in all our ways; that our angels' hands will bear us up, lest we dash our foot against a stone.*

In a book he wrote on angels, Billy Graham wrote: "The most important characteristic of angels is not that they have power to exercise control over our lives, or that they are beautiful, but that they work on our behalf. They are motivated by an inexhaustible love for God and are jealous to see that the will of God in Jesus Christ is fulfilled in us." (Angels, p.56)

My mother wasn't a saint; she may have been even more. To Dr. John, she was someone he asked if he could adopt as his mother (Momma) because his own mother had died while he was in graduate school at UCLA. And certainly, her granddaughter and my daughter, Sarah, knows that her heart for giving and helping others today was nurtured by my mother's genes and her model of generosity toward those less fortunate. *We are blessed to know Mother still lives with us in vivid memories, photos, artwork she created, and in the legacy of her selfless giving that's now blessing the children of many Northern Nevada families and families worldwide who are enjoying one or more of the hundreds of dolls from her extensive doll collection and beanie baby collection that we gave in her name for hundreds of others to enjoy.*

Mother's life message: be generous and celebrate life!

Thanks, Mom!

9

What Do Santa Claus and Christ

Have in Common? Me!

- Passion: While any number of passions may weave in and out of our lives, people who know me well would attest that I'm flat-out passionate about Christ. I love everything about Christ Jesus: talking, praying, loving, reading, and thinking, and almost everything about the subject of Christianity.

- Your passion is a strong emotion and can change the world in which you live and in which you have the opportunity to influence others. *Importantly, when you're operating from passion,* others may be supercharged by your enthusiasm, while others may be offended.

- Your passion will bring you great happiness and joy, a lifestyle of achievement, and a tremendous amount of satisfaction, purpose, and money.

- Your passion is the voice through which you need to speak to the world. It will be at *the heart of your million-dollar dream or at the center of how you will touch millions of people with your ideas and creativity.*

- Happiness: You've given me a unique opportunity to experience joy, perhaps a bit unusual for most folks, but one that truly provides me with a sense of pure bliss when I'm tuned into my passions, one of which is you, Santa!

MY STORY

You got me, Lord—oh, do You have me from Your sacrifice on the cross at Calvary and from the promises offered me in Your Word and throughout my life. You've given me balance inside, and with it, a great energy to do all I do, knowing You're with me all the way.

And Santa, there's no doubt that you came to me as a blessing so very long ago when I needed to know you were more than a doll stuffed in a bright red suit. You've given me a unique opportunity to experience a happiness that's perhaps a bit unusual for most folks, but that truly provides me with a sense of pure bliss.

Santa, you've got to know you are still relevant; when I tune into my passions, I'm quick to recognize the spirit of love, giving, and joy you continue to bring to so many people throughout the world, which still inspires me!

* * * *

How different and how alike the two of them are in my life today: Both are with me always. The Lord is forever in my heart, soul, mind, and in the thoughts and ideas I express. Santa is always strategically placed around my house during the Christmas season. During the rest of the year, all 110 of my replica Santas are carefully packed and stored by

Dr. John in our garage. But again, both Santa and the Lord affect people all over the world in so many similar, yet distinctly different ways...and I love them and all they represent to all who believe in you, Santa!

Indeed, Christ and Santa are but a breath away, and I'd have it no other way! And that's where I've been chided, looked at askance, and even criticized by some folks, yet applauded by others. According to my sound meter, the applause is louder, but the criticisms themselves have long been more biting and distracting, though at times rather hilarious!

You might be asking yourself: Why am I writing about Santa Claus and Christ in the same chapter, and why at all in this book? Good question, and considering the "you're obsessed with Santa" comments I've heard most of my adult life and the sheer nastiness of some of the biting comments I've heard about my openly professed love of Christ and Pentecostal upbringing (e.g., Jesus freak, Holy Roller), I'll be real candid: I do indeed love my Santa Claus collection, and *I'm a lifer with Christ!*

Santa's no fictional creation. His origins are traced to the fourth century in Turkey, when he was known as Saint Nicholas. He was well known for his generosity, giving food and clothes to people in poverty and children. His legend and stories grew throughout the world. Still, essentially, *I have always known Santa to represent the best of loving and giving. He's the paragon of generosity that our hearts emulate during the holiday seasons.* Indeed, Santa is a symbol of loving and universal acceptance— wrapped in a jolly smile!

In our family, trust is a section on how I want my funeral to be handled. Yes, I even planned that, no matter what time of year it is, my collection of 110 Santa Clauses will be proudly displayed around my coffin. I know I will already be with Christ in His Kingdom, but I want the joy Santa brings to so many to be one of the final messages I send to my friends, family, and loved ones. To be sure, Santa is a secular reminder of Christmas. However, we realize that

Christmas is genuinely about the unconditional love of Christ Jesus, born to humankind, that we might have salvation and life eternal with our Savior in heaven!

Okay, okay...I'm caught in a double-bind here: I laugh and roll my eyes when my deeply religious friends try to convince me I am making a disrespectful Christmas case— that Christmas is not about Santa Claus at all, but strictly about the ultimate gift of God, His son Jesus. Still, I must attest this Jesus freak and Holy Roller loves both Christ and Santa Claus, and is quite comfortable with their close yet distinct purposes in my life.

How sad that people miss the point of fantasy, imagery, and surreal characterizations altogether. Remember Dorothy in the Wizard of Oz, how she took on the Wicked Witch of the East and confounded the Wizard himself? Isn't it true that today, when we see a rainbow, we often think of where that place is over the rainbow where our dreams come true? (Visit *www.dreamsfoundationinc.com* for a taste of the sounds of "Over the Rainbow")

Think about how wildly enthusiastic we as a sporting public become over our athletes: we paint our bodies, tear off our clothing, streak stadiums, scream all sorts of nonsense, and then crash. Bottom line, let's back off from judging the painted bodies and those who streak stadiums, and let's donate all those stripped off clothes to charity. If we can't see this otherwise, some might argue we're hung up on pure idol worship!

For me, I worship God the Father, Jesus Christ His Son, and the Holy Spirit—and okay, yes, I really love Santa Claus. Fact is, all our friends know that the only man I'd leave Dr. John for is Santa Claus (I think that's why Dr. John takes such great care of Santa during the storage months to show me how much he appreciates Santa and loves me). That's it, Santa. I've made our relationship public!

LET'S LIGHT UP THE PASSION IN OUR LIVES

Life is about passion and our freedom to be passionate about how we live and interact in this fascinating world into which we've been born. While any number of passions may weave in and out of our lives, people who know me well would attest that I'm flat-out passionate about Christ. I love everything about Christ: talking, praying, loving, reading, and thinking—and almost everything about the subject of Christianity. And the truth of the matter is that I take plenty of crap for it—some blatant, some under the breath, truly insidious. And you know what, this motivates me even more because it's here that I know how deep, compelling, and true my passion for Christ is as it churns about in my belly, always hungry for more. Can I get an Amen?

When you are speaking, teaching, leading, orchestrating, or charting a course for others to follow, the essential word is "passion." Your passion is a strong emotion that can change the world you live in and the opportunities you have to influence others. Importantly, when you're operating from passion, others may be super-charged by your enthusiasm , while others may be offended. The former will ignite you even more; the latter will let you know what they think, but give them a chance to receive the message your passion carries!

Know that God imbued your life with different aspects of passion: 1) a passion to express your thoughts, ideas, visions, and intentions through music; 2) a passion to be creative in expressing your thoughts and ideas in writing; 3) a passion for creative storytelling; 4) a passion for delivering a passionate message through art, music, photography, drama, etc.? Think of your friends and family: do they all have your passions, and if so, do they express them similarly, or do they have their own passions?

Three of my husband's passions include writing, weightlifting, and golfing (change that to skiing and snowboarding in the winter). Three of my daughter's passions are creating art, entertaining, and photography. Yet we all come from the same household!

People may not understand your passions at first or at all; no matter, it is essential that you know and understand them. Really, most people don't think about you as you think they might. Eleanor Roosevelt explained this well: "You wouldn't worry so much about what others think of you if you realized how seldom they do."

So, let me return this story to where I began. Reflecting over my life, I have sat on Santa's lap and kissed his cheek throughout my childhood and into adulthood, having had Santa visit many of my Christmas office parties—and yes, I have many pictures immortalizing the moments. I still receive Santa letters (source not always known) and post them in my office. Yes, when my husband and I set out the 110 Santa Clauses at Christmas time, I kiss each one of them on the cheek, welcoming them into our home. I'm free to do so because I'm free to believe and to express my beliefs. We all need that freedom!

Similarly, I was born into my love affair with Christ. Frankly, I know no other way. He has been with me every day of my life. He dwells within me. He talks and walks with me. My faith in God and Christ and the Holy Spirit is as One—a Triune God!

Your passion is the voice through which you need to speak to the world. It will be at the *heart of your million-dollar dream or at the center of how you will touch millions of people with your ideas and creativity!* Your passion will bring you great happiness and joy, a lifestyle of achievement, and a tremendous amount of satisfaction, purpose, and money! So, discover your passion and step into your greatness!

CHALLENGES I OVERCAME

It was late in the year 2009, and earlier in the year, I had opened my first real estate brokerage. It was truly an exciting time in my real estate career, during which I did very well as a realtor working for a local Reno real estate company. I was now ready to charge into the marketplace. My success had been primarily due to my early positioning in the distressed real estate market and to building a small team of young, passionate, and energetic realtors, including my daughter, Sarah. I had established a versatile practice with a host of banks, asset management companies, and governmental housing agencies.

Additionally, I had a good inventory of traditional houses for sale, and my team hustled to sell the properties I listed and those of other realtors. You know, I love to read, and coincidentally, Christmas was drawing near; of course, it was Santa Claus time, and as we were planning our festivities, I noticed this old real estate how-to book that Dr. John and I had from our early days of real estate investing. The book was an '80s book written by a woman CEO with some gutsy ideas for marketing her business. One of her articles particularly caught my attention. *Coincidentally, there was a solicitation on the streets* (i.e., a competitive real estate company bidding process) for a prized government housing agency contract in our state and locale.

I'm no dummy: 1+1 = 2, and that book I read had a truly goofy, but very definite solicitation idea in it. So, what the heck, what could I lose? The premise was simply this: the author sent a single nice tennis shoe to a potential contract company with her business cards and other identifying materials, and used the theme: "Just wanted to get my foot in the door so we could meet and talk."

Well, I saw this and decided to take it a step further. *Instead of a tennis shoe, I sent a golden high-heeled shoe!* With it, I'd make a similar, "Just wanted to get my foot in the door" ploy, but then added something like, "Let's not pass up this golden opportunity to meet and talk about what my golden team has to offer—we take no prisoners, and we commit the resources needed to manage and sell your homes and real property assets!"

Again, this was a very high-profile government housing agency, but I was operating out of a passion mindset. So off went the packaged golden high heel shoe and a completed application and contract assurance. It had been several days, and we had expected at least a phone call or e-mail, but nothing.

Ugh, okay, I was human.

Admittedly, I was mega-pumped and excitedly anticipating phone contact with the project officer, and, as irony would have it, I phoned in accordance with agency protocol. The operator at the agency end asked me to hold while I was transferred to the project officer's secretary.

"Hi, it's Mr. Jackson; can I help you?"

Yikes, Mr. Jackson was the dude I had sent the golden high heel shoe to. I caught my breath briefly and offered: "So, Mr. Jackson, do you like gold?"

His response wasn't what I'd hoped for. "You're the off-the-wall broker with a foot fetish. Sorry, ma'am, didn't work for me or anyone else here at ABC." He paused for a moment. "Some of us found that package flat out insulting. This is a national housing business, not a fashion boutique!"

"Well," I said assertively, "do I get a chance at this contract?" Frankly, with the level of passion coursing through my bloodstream, I never bought into his panning of my golden high heel shoe ploy.

"We've got a lot of fine candidates," he said. "I'm not sure many wear gold colored high heel shoes." He coughed as if to clear his throat and added, "This really is a practical joke, yes?"

"No, I'm dead serious about my offer."

"Okay, ma'am, I think I'm getting that, but I'm not sure my boss is going to look at this the same way." "Will you promise me he'll at least see it?"

He paused, then said, "You're gutsy; okay, I'll make sure he knows it's for real."

I haven't lost my passion, but about then I felt like a pawn in a chess game, with no move to make. But I remember Dr. John telling me one time, it's not always so bad feeling like a pawn in a chess game, because depending on how your opponents move their chess pieces, your little pawn can place their King in checkmate. Okay, game on!

I heard nothing from anyone for several days, and the bid deadline was a couple of days away. It was Friday midday , and my office received a phone call from Mr. Jackson's office.

"Yes, yes, put him through to my office," I said to my office manager.

"Hi, Mr. Jackson, this is Terry."

"Terry Rasner-Yacenda? Hi, this is Mr. Jackson's wife calling. I just wanted to tell you personally that your proposal was well thought out, had good budget numbers, and you appeared to have the right staff and local reputation to pull it off. There is just one thing I had a question about: Do the golden high heels fit you?"

I paused, a bit off guard, and answered this very soft-spoken woman, "Why yes, they do." Then she went on to tell me to be sure to wear a pair of golden high-heeled shoes to our first agency's contractors' meeting to add a little class to the contracting corps!

Kudos to my team at Reno/Tahoe Realty Group, LLC. Although we're a new master contractor, we received the annual contract for a fifth year running. We haven't had to box another shoe since then, *though I'm sure we would if the need were apparent!*

OVERCOMING THE CHALLENGES

The passion that drives me is drawn from my relationship with Our Lord Jesus Christ. As I've stated in this chapter, it's been lifelong. I'm only fooling myself and others if I deny it or suggest in some obscure way that it's all about my abilities and talents because it's really all about the skills and divine opportunities I've been given to arrange, coalesce, and manifest into who I've become as a She Is All Business businesswoman.

The big vision of She Is All Business is one of a thriving entrepreneurial company focused primarily on women - a company whose CEO looks first to God, and then moves in accordance with the urgings of His Holy Spirit. This businesswoman will be the catalyst to creating your million-dollar dream (and then helping you bring it to life!). She is a dream-maker who's not afraid to pray or take risks of faith, and she's an expert at using both radical and unconventional methods and systems for personal and business applications.

When you embrace her creative spirit as nurtured by her faith in God, neither *she nor God will ever disappoint you.* However, you may find yourself going in a different direction than you planned. Understand, this Holy Spirit–inspired businesswoman appears at times to have the will of a wild mustang, unbridled, untamed, and free. *She will take you to your highest level of self-mastery...if you give her the reins! She is the persona of supernatural and extraordinary strength—give her a try, and know that if you're right with God, you can be certain He's got your back.*

Carry this lasting image in your mind and embrace the essence *She Is All Business* brings to your life; hold on and give her the reins! See yourself as God's Intern!

YOUR TURN

- When you think Million-Dollar-Dream, what's the first thing that comes to mind?

Don't be shy. This is your million-dollar dream.

- Back to chapter 1: What's something that rocks your socks? (No pet rocks, but maybe rockers for worn-out socks.)

- Why should your Million-Dollar-Dream become a reality (and who will benefit from it)?

APPLYING TRANSFORMATIONAL THINKING (TT) TO YOUR LIFE TODAY

Are you ready to get your She Is All Business headset on and give yourself the reins to take you to that place of Passion where God wants you to be?

- Prove your identity or ideology through your work.

- Broadcast what you believe in or stand for when allowed to do so.

- Hear me - I'm a Jesus freak, Holy Roller, and *lifer with Christ—it's my conviction!*

- I have a "Ho Ho, Jolly St. Nick" relationship with a stuffed Santa!

- Find as many creative and practical ways as you can to express your passion and invite others into your modes of expression so they, too, may sample or taste a bit of the passion you feel.

- Be intentional with your passion(s) and enlist others to share your passion(s) by inviting them into your world to participate in the exercise of your passion(s) in different venues; this is the fun stuff and serious plans you have for changing the world in which you live!

- Your ultimate passion will be at the heart of your million-dollar dream. It will bring you great happiness and joy, a lifestyle of achievement, and a tremendous amount of satisfaction and purpose in living!

10

My Hunka Wunka!

There's a very good reason this chapter is the last one in my book, and the general organizational theme I've used for the previous chapters just doesn't fit anymore. You see, this chapter is about the man who's had a tremendous impact on my career choices, life with my mother during the most tragic post-accident years of her life, and who currently stands at the ready to assist me when trouble looms, prays for me when it's the touch of God I most need for healing, be daddy to our dog, Truffles, and grandpa to Sarah's dog, Stallone, tend to our fruit and vegetable garden in the backyard, and to stay out of my way when I'm mad at him!

Yes, that last one's tough, but life's not always easy for either of us since a once fateful Saturday in March of 2011, when Dr. John suffered a stroke and fell to the floor in our home office , sweating profusely, lying there as we awaited the arrival of an ambulance. A week of hospitalization and testing confirmed the stroke; his life, my life, our life has forever changed! Even as I type this, I am aware that when this book goes to print, Dr. John may not be around to enjoy its reception. Still, it's just as likely he'll go on tour with me to promote the book and the company, She Is All Business!

LIVING TO DIE OR DYING TO LIVE

This is the dilemma we face in our life together; it's the challenge I must face daily. I think you can understand: I don't know from one day to the next if Dr. John is living and getting ready to die or dying a little bit each day, yet holding on to life because he wants to live it as fully as possible.

When you look at Dr. John on the surface, you see a very tan, muscular, well-built man with a full moustache, great white smile, and full head of hair that hasn't started graying. While he's well over fifty, pegging his age is not easy when you look at him, particularly when he's wearing a tank top and doing a weightlifting workout in our community gym. The same thing's pretty much true when you watch him golfing, skiing, or snowboarding—he doesn't look or act his age!

There are even more ironies when he's wearing a suit and tie and parading through the Nevada Legislature, Governor's Office, or lecturing in any number of settings. He doesn't look like he's dying, but we both know he is living with a death sentence.

I believe his cardiologist was the first specialist who didn't bother to reschedule another visit after two years of follow-up visits; other specialists don't even maintain contact.

BATTLEING THE DOCS AND MEDS

Something that's been important to us and where we've stood together is standing up to doctors who made premature doom-and-gloom assumptions and taking a stand against medical prescriptions that seemed to have more adverse side effects than benefits. It was challenging for me to watch my Dr. John become a pharmacological zombie over ill-advised prescriptions that just weren't right for him. And I'll tell you not every prescription is written correctly in terms of dosage and dosage frequency; when you really read about the prescriptions, you'll be better armed to challenge the doctors, and there are times they must be challenged—and times you must insist the medications be changed!

WHAT'S REALLY BEHIND THE CURTAINS

These are some of the hardest observations, now realities, that now define our post-stroke lives. Dr. John has always been a patient husband, easy to talk to, and a tremendous listener. What you can't see behind the tan, great build, and inviting smile is that the stroke disrupted Dr. John's psyche. He's not the same patient husband; he's often more argumentative in conversations, more openly opinionated, and doesn't listen as well as he once did. It's like he's afraid "his time" (to live and enjoy life) is being taken away from him.

Fact is, his easygoing demeanor has become grumpy, contentious, and a bit argumentative around the people who know him the best. I want to understand it was the stroke that caused these changes, but these changes are nonetheless unsettling.

The way my mind works, the more these altered demeanor items occur in his life, the closer he becomes to simply checking out, but then he'll take on a new project or have a near under-par round of golf or great ski race result. I'm back at point zero—although I do have to remember that after the stroke, it took him a couple of years before he could again play his guitar or powerfully swing a golf club. It's really a mind twister for me; how much of his athletic potential was lost to the stroke, and what has he reclaimed through his stubborn tenacity?

The worst of psyche disruptions that have become part of post-stroke Dr. John are those that invade what I once described as "the fire that burns deeply within us"—referring to our seventeen years together, during which we've stood grounded and through our marriage have shared a common thread explaining our love of God and people through which we have expressed our passions and charted our destiny.

So, my reality, even as I launched She Is All Business several years ago, was that while Dr. John had a passion for my work and had always said I needed to do this, would he still be with me as the business developed?

Surprise? No, not really. This is my book's Second Edition. Dr. John is golfing better than ever, skiing like an adult kid on the wild side, and still benching 260+lb as part of his routine weightlifting workout. Alas, the grumpy, contentious, and a bit argumentative demeanor linger, all grim reminders of that horrible evening in March 2011.

I am a bit better at living with the reality that my life is clouded with the imponderable: Will I be with Dr. John next month, or next year? I know the reality: it wasn't just that he had a stroke in March of 2011, but two years later, he almost died from internal bleeding, unrelated to the stroke, but related to a blood clot in his leg.

Churches and ministers all over the world prayed for him to get through the internal bleeding; he did and has never had the problem again. But I must be realistic, as there are multiple doctor visits and hospital stays, though both are now infrequent, today there are still blood stains on pillow cases, bloody noses that last anywhere from 3-20 hours in duration, easy bleeding, bruising, and even black eyes of unknown origin.

At first, I felt worry and confusion, then a bit of resentment and anger—why me? Why us? All of it was greatly relieved when I accepted the obvious: I had to give it all over to God. He would call the shots, and I had to place my faith and trust in Him. In truth, the feeling was liberating for me, and I realized Dr.

John had long ago given it to God and insisted on living and *is comfortable with dying to live!*

We spend our days like other couples, working at our offices (which are located on each of the two floors in the same commercial building we own), sharing, cleaning, walking the dog, and assorted other activities. But the truth be known, before I came to this sense of peace in God with the state of Dr. John's health, I was in constant turmoil with an agony gripping me that Dr. John was going to die!

It is difficult to quiet the theater of your mind, and mine was daily rehearsing the ending of Dr. John's life. The questions that arose: will he die in his sleep, will he die at the gym, will he collapse on a walking path? This was constantly playing in the theater of my mind, fueling my insane thoughts. When my faith is weak, I am exhausted from life's demands, and it's not surprising when others use my weakness to project their negativity on me; I often permit it to take root.

So, my success in living in this bleak environment of sadness, worry, and despair is my incredible faith in God, doing everything physically productive, and following healthy, common-sense best practices. We stay committed and focused, with the confidence to make changes as needed.

OVERCOMING THE CHALLENGES

It's hard to wrap our minds around my post-stroke Dr. John. This man looks 15 years younger than his real age. He works out with weights three days a week: bench pressing 260 for the last five reps of his 20,000 lb bench routine, followed by an abdominal pull-down workout in which he moves 15,000 pounds, and concludes with a bicep curl exercise where he bar-curls a total of 2100 pounds. Then on his non-gym days, he goes golfing, skis, or snowboards. Fortunately, there are no more triathlons in his life.

The big problem (or conundrum I face emotionally) is that people who know his story don't believe for one minute he is living to die; should I bother to explain he is , or   defer to the writing on the wall that says with certainty that in Dr. John's mind, he's dying to live and running our lives as if he is. Maybe this book will be the path to my joining the "dying to live" team?

It's now to the point that no doctors remind him it's time to check in with them, and his primary care physician sends him lab orders when he needs a series of tests. As far as dentists and ophthalmologists, Dr. John goes to them when he needs them. Generally, Dr. John reduces his blood-thinning medication before any dental work or invasive testing. However, besides the day-to-day bumps and bruises, we decided to stop visiting doctors with "ologists" in their titles, ever since his hematologist reviewed his blood work and tests over a year ago and said, "Nothing more we can do; go enjoy your life!"

And darn it, that's just what Dr. John is doing, and I just haven't been able to join the dying to live team fully!

Nonetheless, I've enabled the dying to live lifestyle by stopping the nagging about you can't do this or that. I knew it was hopeless on my part when, during his final visit with his cardiologist, the doctor lectured Dr. John a bit about his weightlifting practices, to which Dr. John yelled back at him: "You expect me to stop doing everything that brings me pleasure in life and just stay home and do nothing." Pregnant pause. "No way, Doc!"

Okay, so I agree with my husband on this one: should he sit around and stop living to wait for his inevitable death? I think that day I got it, although I still need to turn my head the other way when I hear of some of the things he's doing, done, or words he's said. He's just got to understand that my worry and fear will not change the situation; maybe he's dying to live...a bit arrogantly?

I must say this with strength and conviction: Dr. John and I are not victims—we must stand together in refusing to nurse and rehearse the hopeless situation. The other option could well be a hearse, and he has motion sickness. Join me and curse the post-stroke condition. Join our commitment to our faith in God and marching in His army of life. Admittedly, the disease may win a permanent victory in having a claim on Dr. John's life, *but we (Dr. John with me by his side) are winning the battle to stay in the game of life!*

REFLECTIONS

We're a quirky couple; yes, we're real, and I might add we've developed some long-surviving habits: buying cards for each other for different occasions (and including cards from our pet dogs as well to Mommy and Daddy); going dancing at clubs, spontaneously dancing in our living room, dancing at weddings, dancing in the car, or wherever; we pray for each other for healing, worry, fear or doubt; and we talk, give each other the silent treatment, grunt, and moan (ahh, mainly Dr. John), we verbally fight, we dream and dream, and to tell the truth, the best thing we do together is push the envelope as far as we can and will until Dr. John dies.

My final words of Transformational Thinking for Your Life: Live like you know you are dying— that is, live *dying to live* with everything you've got! Write your eulogy, and then go live it! Spend quality time with the ones you love! Stop hesitating; just do it! Dance, kiss, be silly, travel, and mostly, don't stop doing or dreaming!

YOUR TURN

- When you think of your Hunka Wunka, what's the first thing that comes to mind? Don't be shy; there is good and bad.

About She Is All Business

In less than 5 years, with little business experience, I built an 8-figure empire, all because I allowed God to be the CEO...If others can't quite understand your behavior, thinking you're acting a bit out of character, smile and tell them you're listening to the call from your spirit within. You're ready to get on your She Is All Business headset and give her the reins to take you to that place of passion where God wants you to be...pursuing the integrated life changes that'll give you greater access to your God-given talents, gifts, and passions!

There are undoubtedly many messages in She Is All Business, but above all...until I understood and believed with all my heart and soul that God was the message of my success and blessings, all the wonderful and exciting concepts I learned about business and people meant little. She Is All Business will help you recognize the work of God in your life through His actions, His words, and the Holy Spirit. For you see - and must know - God is always on the move in our lives; make way for his leadership, and your life as an entrepreneur and successful business owner will be a witness to how well you listened to and are obedient to God!

About The Author

Terry Rasner is a nationally recognized leader in the real estate industry, a talented public speaker, and an inspirational leader who epitomizes a God-anointed entrepreneurial spirit.

She is the CEO of Capital City Investments Inc., She co-founded Reno/Tahoe Realty Group, LLC., Superpowergirl.com, and She Is All Business – all actively conducting business. Terry resides in Reno, Nevada, with her daughter/business partner, Sarah Carmona Zink, son-in-law, Howard Edward Zink III, and grandson, Howard Edward Zink IV.

www.ingramcontent.com/pod-product-compliance
Lightning Source LLC
Chambersburg PA
CBHW060629130626
46555CB00002B/719